Lucky Girl

Unveiling the Secrets of Manifesting a Lucky Life

T0050058

Georgie May

CAPSTONE
A Wiley Brand

Registered Office(s)
John Wiley & Sons Ltd, The Atrium, Southern Gate, Chichester, West Sussex, PO19 8SQ, UK
John Wiley & Sons, Inc., 111 River Street, Hoboken, NJ 07030, USA

For details of our global editorial offices, customer services, and more information about Wiley products visit us at www.wiley.com.

Wiley also publishes its books in a variety of electronic formats and by print-on-demand. Some content that appears in standard print versions of this book may not be available in other formats.

Library of Congress Cataloging-in-Publication Data is Available:

ISBN: 9781394230693(paperback)
ISBN: 9781394230785(epdf)
ISBN: 9781394230778(epub)

Cover Design: Kathy Davis
Cover Images: © VolodymyrSanych/Shutterstock, © Love the wind/Shutterstock

SKY10065174_011724

To all the Lucky Girls.

To the dreamers, the doers, and the believers—this book is for you. May the tools, techniques, and insights within these pages empower you to shape your destiny, attract positivity, and manifest your desires. May you find the strength to navigate the challenges and embrace all the opportunities that come your way.

To those who have supported me on my journey to share this knowledge, to my husband, family, friends, mentors, and readers—your encouragement and belief in the power of luck have fuelled my passion to create this guide.

And to the future Lucky Girls who will turn these pages, may you find inspiration, transformation, and the keys to unlock the door to a life filled with abundant luck, success, and happiness. You truly deserve it.

With gratitude and excitement,

Georgie

Contents

Acknowledgments

As I reflect on this incredible journey that led to the creation of *Lucky Girl*, I am profoundly grateful for the unwavering support and love I have received from the remarkable people in my life. This book is a testament to the power of community, and I am fortunate beyond measure to have such an extraordinary network of individuals who have walked this path alongside me.

First and foremost, I am blessed to call my family my greatest source of inspiration and strength. To my amazing mother, my best friend, and my role model, your guidance, wisdom, and boundless love have shaped me in ways I could never adequately express. You are my Lucky Girl role model – teaching me from the start that with hard work, patience, courage, and kindness, we can achieve anything. Without you, these words would not exist, I wouldn't exist, and for that, I am endlessly thankful.

My father, with his relentless drive and tenacity, has shown me that luck is not a mere roll of the dice but a product of hard work and determination. Your journey from humble beginnings to creating your own luck has been a guiding light in my life, reminding me of the power of resilience and always striving to be the best version of yourself.

To my incredible brother and sister, your unwavering dedication and unbreakable spirit inspire me daily. Your tireless support and infectious laughter have carried me through the toughest times, and I am grateful to both for putting up with my sh*t.

A special mention goes to my extraordinary husband, whose presence in my life has been nothing short of a stroke of luck. From a drunken night at the office to a whirlwind romance. Together, we have built a beautiful life filled with love, joy, and endless possibilities. Your unwavering belief in me has been my driving force, and I am privileged to have you by my side.

I am profoundly thankful for my circle of wonderful friends, the ones who have been my pillars of strength throughout this adventure. Your constant encouragement, genuine camaraderie, and unwavering support have meant the world to me. You know who you are, and I am grateful for every moment shared.

To Laura Galebe, affectionately known as the CEO of the 'Memoir Technique,' and Sammy K, and all those who saw Lucky Girl Syndrome as more than a bandwagon. Your collective influence in popularising this transformative trend cannot be overstated. The courage you display in sharing your personal experiences is what ignited a spark within me to delve deeper into the concept of Lucky Girl Syndrome and write a book about it.

A heartfelt thank you to Annie, my editor, the amazing Alice, and the incredible team at John Wiley & Sons. Your expertise, dedication, and belief in this project have been instrumental in bringing *Lucky Girl* to life. Your collaboration has been invaluable, and I am truly honoured to have worked with you.

In closing, I extend my deepest appreciation to each and every person who has played a role in shaping this book and my journey. Your presence has been a stroke of luck beyond measure, and I am humbled by your unwavering support.

With heartfelt gratitude,

Georgie

About the Author

Georgie May, in her transformative journey from a former burnout party girl to a spiritual explorer, struggled for years with poor mental health, desperately seeking a 'magic cure' to alleviate her pain. Like many people, she experimented with various conventional methods, hoping to find a solution. Eventually, she opened up to alternative paths, leading her into the wonderful, if often weird, world of wellness.

Leaving behind her 9–5 job at a major social media marketing agency, Georgie immersed herself in the realm of wellness. She earned certifications in EFT tapping, yoga, and reflexology, establishing her own business with a mission to guide others in their healing. Through workshops, events, classes, and private sessions, she has appreciated the privilege of working with a diverse range of clients, gaining deep insights into their unique perspectives and challenges.

In addition to her personal journey, Georgie became committed to dismantling the stigma around mental health. Drawing inspiration from ancient practices and modern psychology, her work focuses on the intersection of spirituality, mental health, and self-discovery. This commitment led her to write *Lucky Girl*, a book born out of her desire to extend a lifeline to others navigating life's challenges and the minefield of advice.

In *Lucky Girl*, Georgie shares the wisdom gained from her odyssey toward self-discovery, offering practical insights and empowering narratives. She firmly believes that luck is not a matter of chance but a state of being, a mindset cultivated through resilience and self-compassion. Through her book, she aims to empower readers to rewrite their own narratives, emphasising that luck is about mindset, intention, and self-belief.

Georgie's hope is that *Lucky Girl* becomes a companion for anyone striving to create a life filled with purpose, joy, and authentic connection. Her aspiration is to inspire a ripple effect of positivity, kindness, and self-love, where everyone feels deserving of the incredible blessings life has to offer.

Preface

What happens when 'The Secret' meets Social Media?

A new manifestation trend is born:

Lucky Girl Syndrome

'I'm so lucky, everything works out for me' – an optimistic thought process or a totally delusional one?

This book will blow the lid off Lucky Girl Syndrome and teach you how to harness this approach to attract the life you desire . . . *without sounding like a total spoilt bitch.*

I know what you are thinking, and I'm thinking it too: how sad that a grown-ass woman who's just turned 30 is wasting their precious time mindlessly scrolling on an app they are way too old to be on in the first place . . .

Well, I do this daily for a few reasons:

1. I like looking at pretty, aesthetically pleasing things.

2. Part of my line of work requires me to be on social media.

3. I feel it's my duty as a millennial to at least try to keep up with the trends and stay cool for the younger generation.

4. I have ADHD, so my short attention span loves to feed off this short-form content.

5. Videos of people doing silly things and cute dogs will never not be entertaining for me.

In essence, a large portion of my time is spent online.

Hi, I'm Georgie, and I'm a social media addict.

And I'll first admit to this – I've absolutely wasted hours of my time scrolling and countless times have been sucked into the dark side, where social media can make you feel totally sh*t about yourself and stuck in the comparison trap. When you see others living the most incredible lives, doing things you could only have ever dreamt of, going to beautiful places, and achieving brilliant things – making you feel inadequate, lacking, and jealous.

Now, it's not just social media that can make you feel that way, but it sure does have a lot to answer for. With the rise and emergence of new online platforms, we all possess this intrinsic need to be on them and share parts of our lives with the world. The two driving forces behind sharing are status and emotion – it doesn't matter which sharing persona you fit, the basic psychology behind why we share is because of these two factors.

Social media is an emotional rollercoaster. I'll be belly laughing at a prank, irate at a DM asking me to join their pyramid scheme, swooning over my many celebrity crushes, crying at a friend's baby, and disgusted at some ignorant trolls – and that can all be in the space of 10 minutes. Like Marmite, social media is a divisive experience: you either love it or hate it. Regardless of your stance, there's no denying that it has become a significant part of our pastime, and it's clear that it's here to stay.

And I'm grateful it is. Without it, I wouldn't have ended up on 'SpiritualTok' – and when something inside me really shifted and from that mindless scrolling session, I found my new life's mantra:

I am a Lucky Girl.

_____

Just like that, from that one TikTok video – from there on out, I've made it my life's mission to live every day in full awareness of how lucky I am and share the gift of luck with everyone.

_____

Yes, there were times when I haven't been so lucky and certainly times when I have really struggled; the bullies at school, the abusive relationships, the depressive episodes, the countless rejections, and the times when I felt truly so unlucky, I tried to escape this lucky life. But my god how lucky am I to not only have survived these traumatic events but to have come back fighting each time, more and more determined to live my life in a meaningful and authentic way and – be a Lucky Girl.

Despite being a Lucky Girl, even now I still get 'down days' and of course, know I'll still meet many bumps along the road, but what has always got me through is a constant reminder to come back to being fully present at the moment, no matter how difficult it is, and acknowledge even the smallest of luck in my every day with a sense of deep and profound gratitude. Now, it's certainly not easy to do, and requires a lot of bloody hard work, but if you're ready to start harnessing the power of luck to attract more in your life, then prepare to get uncomfortable, start to become open and get ready to switch up your mindset as this is where the magic of lasting change will happen.

Through the strategies outlined in this book, I've managed to create a great deal of luck for myself, and I've designed a life that a younger me could only have ever dreamt of by making shifts that can change my perspective in a split second and reconnect me back to my core self.

BIG, big shifts, actually. Shifts I want to share with you now . . .

The Lucky Girl Contract

I _____ hereby declare:

I will use my Lucky Girl powers for good. I will share my knowledge of this practice with all around me because I know there is more than enough to go around for everyone.

I understand luck is no coincidence, however, I realise it is up to me to find it, create it, and sustain it.

I am fully committed to the hard work that is needed for my luck to work.

I understand that lucky girl syndrome won't solve my problems, but learning this new approach may help me react in a more positive and healthier way.

I will celebrate all the lucky milestones I reach – big or small.

All the luck I receive I will share back out, fully knowing there is more than enough to go around.

From here on out, I acknowledge that I am a lucky girl.

Signed _____

Date _____

1

What Is Lucky Girl Syndrome?

We've all been there – the alarm goes off late (or you forgot to even set it!), you're already late for work, and you haven't even had your morning wee. No clean knickers because you forgot to do the laundry. Morning commute hasn't gone to plan and it's pouring with rain which means your bra is showing through your now wet shirt, resulting in disapproving looks from the HR manager. Then you realise that the proposal you spent hours working on didn't save correctly. Fast forward, the day goes from bad to worse.

What sh*t luck.

This may be followed with other negative inner chatter such as 'Why do bad things always happen to me?', 'Nothing goes my way', or, my personal favourite, 'Just my f*cking luck'.

On the flip side, we've all been there – you wake up to birdsong and sunshine. It's Saturday, so you can have an extra hour in bed if desired. You go for brunch with girls, and they all compliment you on the promotion you got yesterday. The guy who's been on your radar for some time drops into your DMs and wants to take you out tonight, and you walk past a shop window with the perfect date night outfit . . . and it's on sale!

What great luck!

Now your possible positive inner chatter might be 'Isn't it funny how life works out for me?', 'Everything is going my way right now', or, my personal favourite, 'How f*cking lucky am I?'

But that's life, right? The ups and downs are part of an individual's everyday life, no?

Indeed, it is, but maybe there's something more to it?

What initially started from two girls eating noodles in a car, detailing their experience with this 'bulletproof' theory, quickly turned into a viral sensation, amassing over 400 million views since publication and thousands across the globe engaging in the trend.

The noodle girls believe it's as simple as shifting your thoughts from negative to positive. Sounds simple – and if TikTok says it works, then that means it must do – right?!

But is it just a TikTok trend that seemingly gives the entitled yet another platform to show off, or could there actually be something in this line of thinking?

Can this 'syndrome' be adopted by *all*, despite an individual's background?

Could a simple hashtag actually help make meaningful and lasting changes in our lives?

Are these life events coincidences or just luck? Reactions from social media seem to think it's worth a shot . . .

First and foremost, to be clear – this isn't a term I've originated, nor am I claiming it as my own. No, no – the term *Lucky Girl Syndrome* was first coined by Laura Galebe, CEO of the Memoir Technique, and TikTok influencer. Galebe created a video in which she described her own experience with the syndrome, and the video quickly went viral.

And if you are not on TikTok, that's OK, we will get you up to speed. Or if you are a seasoned scroller and totally up to date with what we're harping on about, I encourage you to still read this chapter because we will be going one step further, as your social sisters are only telling you half the story.

Whoever you are, wherever you are, please read this book with an open mind and an open heart as we unpack what this technique is, dispel the misconceptions, take a deeper dive into the science, the case studies, and ultimately help you to apply the learnings in your everyday life.

Stumbling upon a post related to Lucky Girl Syndrome (LGS) and feeling the urge to commence anew can be exhilarating. However, approach your luck journey with a well-rounded understanding of psychology, science, and the core concept itself, to then integrate these insights seamlessly into your daily existence. This is the primary objective of this book – to guide you through the process, not to just dive blindly into manifestation but to equip you with the necessary tools and knowledge.

Comprehending LGS establishes a strong base. This foundation empowers you to approach manifestation with insight and intention, rather than haste. This journey is more about gradual evolution than shortcuts. Let it be clear that this book doesn't profess to be a miraculous remedy that will completely heal all wounds. You're going to have to do the work – embrace the wisdom within this book, align your actions and thoughts, and you will witness meaningful transformations over time.

In essence, this book bridges theory and practice, guiding you to unlock your potential through understanding LGS. As you embark on this enlightening path, embrace learning and growth, creating a life of purpose, success, and true fulfilment.

So let's get into it:

> Lucky Girl Syndrome: A state of mind in which you believe that you are lucky and that good things are more likely to happen to you. It is based on the idea that positive thinking can attract positive experiences.

The whole premise of Lucky Girl Syndrome is about attitude. Consistently believing you are fortunate or privileged in various aspects of your life can draw favourable circumstances or experiences. This could include having financial stability, good looks, a loving family, popularity, and being successful or happy. Those with Lucky Girl Syndrome may often perceive themselves as being blessed or fortunate and may be perceived as having an optimistic outlook on life.

This form of 'manifestation' and 'positive thinking' has arguably worked well for many (hello – 400 million views!). Lucky Girl Syndrome – which, despite the name, is not only for girls – gives a strong sense of belief and trust that everything will work out in your favour because you believe you are indeed a lucky person.

If you haven't already heard on social media, 'I'm so lucky; everything works out for me' – then your algorithm sucks, or you're probably doing something more productive with your life than scrolling. Regardless, if you haven't come across this affirmation, then you've been seriously missing out on this latest manifestation technique, and more importantly, you could be missing out on creating your dream life!

Laura Galebe and Sammy K (another TikToker) pushed Lucky Girl Syndrome into the spotlight, sharing their personal experiences trying it out and demonstrating how it completely changed their lives by helping them attract unbelievable outcomes and opportunities.

Manifesting Has Had a Makeover

You're probably thinking about now – isn't this just a wolf wearing 'manifesting' sheep's clothing? Correct, it is.

There are tons of manifesting tools and techniques available. LGS is just the latest craze.

These techniques are often associated with the 'New Thought Movement', a spiritual philosophy that emphasises the power of the mind. This movement, founded in the late nineteenth century by Phineas Quimby, has since been popularised by authors, teachers, and influential people.

The Law of Attraction is the most popular technique – the belief behind the concept is that by focusing on positive thoughts and feelings, you can attract positive experiences into your life. This belief is based on the idea that thoughts are a form of energy and that like energy attracts like. So if you focus on positive thoughts, you will attract positive experiences and, vice versa, focusing on negative thoughts will attract negative experiences.

You may have read the incredible book *The Secret*, by Rhonda Byrne, which gets into the nitty-gritty of the Law of Attraction, explaining it in a comprehensive and informative manner. For me, it's The Bible of Manifestation and if you are new to the world of manifesting, *The Secret* is a fantastic place to start. The book argues that the Law of Attraction is a universal law that applies to everyone, and has helped millions since its publication, who claim Byrne's words of wisdom have created positive change in their lives – proving that the Law of Attraction is more than wishful thinking.

You may even be familiar with the lesser known *The Law of Assumption* (the little sister of the Law of Attraction) by Neville Goddard, who emphasises the power of thoughts and beliefs and thinks LGS is just the latest interpretation of that concept.

Goddard maintained that what we assume to be true, we call into our reality. This law uses imagination as the catalyst for realising our dreams and aspirations and is based on the idea that our reality is created by our thoughts and beliefs. When we assume something to be true, we are essentially programming our subconscious mind to believe that it is true. This belief then manifests itself in our reality.

For example, if you assume you are 'wealthy' you will start to see opportunities to make money. You may start to feel more confident and capable, making it easier for you to achieve your financial goals. When we act as though what we want is already our reality – and believe it – then we are rewarded with the things that we most desire in life.

What Lucky Girl inherently does differently is that it simplifies manifestation by breaking it down into practical steps that anyone can follow. Instead of focusing solely on visualisation and positive thinking, Lucky Girl emphasises the importance of taking action and setting clear intentions. By providing a structured approach to manifestation, it helps individuals navigate the process more effectively and achieve their desired outcomes with greater ease.

Here is a comparison of the basic features of the techniques:

Concept	Definition	Belief
Law of Attraction	The belief that by focusing on positive thoughts and feelings, you can attract positive experiences into your life.	Like attracts like. What you think about, you bring about.
Law of Assumption	The belief that by assuming that something is already true, you can make it become true.	You create your own reality through your thoughts and beliefs.
Lucky Girl	A belief that by simply believing that you are lucky, you will attract good things into your life.	The universe is rigged in your favour.

These techniques use a type of 'you-are-what-you-think' ideology, which is very persuasive and popular because it's reminiscent of ancient wisdom. Read any text of stoic philosophy and you will discover that it suggests that the way we think about ourselves and our situations determines our psychological state, not the situation itself. However, unlike stoic philosophy, when examining Lucky Girl content, it does not acknowledge that sometimes things don't go our way, nor address the fact that when this happens, we need to see it as an opportunity to learn and grow.

LGS content sounds oh-so-simple, which for most us is very appealing; however, it is a fundamental flaw of Lucky Girl Syndrome.

Which One Is Right for Me?

There is no right or wrong answer when it comes to choosing between the Law of Attraction, the Law of Assumption, and the Lucky Girl Syndrome – or indeed other techniques. Ultimately, the best way to find out which one is right for you is to experiment and see what works best for you.

All the techniques are closely intertwined, and in order to be Lucky Girl, we'll be using them all alongside other techniques throughout the book, so forget everything you *think* you know about Lucky Girl Syndrome; we are now going to rewrite and create our own narrative.

How Can I Tell if I'm a Lucky Girl?

A pretty easy answer: You can't really.

Luck is subjective and dependent on how an individual sees life. Someone may see surviving a shark attack as lucky. Some may see losing an arm in a shark attack as unlucky. Some might see finding a penny on the street as lucky; others may cross that very street to avoid bad luck after spotting a black kitty cat. Each of us has a different ideation and opinion of what we perceive as 'luck', hence there is no right or wrong answer here. Through extensive research and analysing case studies, interviews, stories, and, undoubtedly, a whole lot of scrolling, this book hones in on certain characteristics a Lucky person presents and acts as a guide for you to adopt and follow.

The signs that you are a Lucky Girl:

- You tend to focus on the positive aspects of your life.

- You believe that good things are more likely to happen to you.

- You are more likely to take risks and put yourself out there.

- You feel grateful for the good things in your life.

- You feel more positive and optimistic.

- You notice more good things happening in your life, i.e. getting a promotion, meeting new people, finding money.

- You take more risks and put yourself out there.

- You expand your horizons, excited to experience new things.

The signs Lucky Girl Syndrome is not working:

- You may not truly believe that you are lucky.

- You may not be taking any action. Lucky Girl Syndrome is not a passive practice. You need to take action in order to see results.

- You may be expecting too much. If you expect good things to happen all the time, you will be disappointed when they do not.

Lucky Life Audit

- Are you reading this book?

  If so, you have a valuable tool at your disposal . . . the power of sight and literacy.

- Did you eat something today? Do you have access to clean water and food?

  One out of eight people in the world suffers from hunger, so if you don't, be thankful that you're not one of them.

(continued)

(*continued*)

Acknowledge the privilege of having these essential resources available at your fingertips.

- Are you stressed?

    Excellent . . . in moderation. You are blessed to be stressed because you are ambitious and aiming to improve your life, not settle. Embrace it as a sign that you're pushing your limits and growing as a person – it's not about striving for stress that will just make you ill, it's about using the stress you are inevitably faced with as a mechanism for action. Diamonds, after all, are formed under pressure.

- Have you experienced failure?

    Failure is your friend. It's a great teacher, and you learn valuable lessons. Perceive failure as an opportunity, not bad luck.

- Are you reflecting right now?

    Just by pausing to evaluate your life, you're already ahead in self-awareness and personal growth.

- Did you wake up today?

    Each new day is a chance to make a positive impact, embrace new opportunities, and appreciate the gift of life.

- Can you breathe easily?

    The simple act of breathing without difficulty is a blessing many don't enjoy.

- Are you pursuing your dreams?

    Even if you're not, the chances are you're about to be . . . that's why you're here, isn't it?

- Can you choose your path?

   The power to make choices and shape your destiny is a privilege not everyone enjoys.

- Are you able to adapt?

   Of course you are – that's why you're here! Your ability to navigate change and uncertainty is a testament to your resilience and growth.

- Have you felt loved today?

   Expressing and receiving love enriches your life in ways that can't be measured.

   If you can say 'yes' to at least one of the above – you're indeed a Lucky Soul! With the audit, count your blessings and acknowledge the positive aspects of your life. Gratitude and perspective can amplify the luck you create and attract.

Decoding the Syndrome's Name

Let's redefine the name Lucky Girl Syndrome.

Two words of the three-word title can be perceived as harmful and discriminatory:

Lucky *Girl* Syndrome

Accepting that while 'Girl' is part of the title, you don't have to be a girl/woman/she/her; this method is inclusive for everyone, and is not discriminatory, although the method is often associated with women.

So despite 'Lucky Girl Syndrome' being used in a gendered way, thus reinforcing stereotypes, it's important we ignore the word 'Girl' from the outset and rather than being put off or offended by the title, simply focus on the power behind the concept.

If LGS is based on the universal idea that positive thinking and beliefs can attract good things into your life – then do just that. Switch to gender-neutral language and see yourself as a 'Lucky Person', 'Lucky One', or 'Lucky Soul' to adopt the mindset.

Lucky Girl *Syndrome*

The term 'syndrome' is often used to describe a medical condition characterised by a set of symptoms, hence it can have negative connotations, suggesting a worrying condition, and the person associated with it could be perceived as 'abnormal'. LGS isn't a medical condition. Harmful implications of the term 'syndrome' could be avoided by using the word 'approach' instead – but maybe has less of a ring or impact!

Disregarding any negative connotations, let's focus on the book's aim, which is to empower.

Words have the power to evoke strong emotions, both positive and negative. Negative words can be particularly powerful because they can trigger our fear, anger, or disgust.

Our cognitive biases influence our perception of words. People are quick to criticise Lucky Girl Syndrome purely based on its name and therefore don't get to know the intention behind the method. By focusing on the negative aspects of the title, you are ignoring the positive aspects – this is known as selective attention. The context in which a word is used can also affect its meaning. For example, the word 'stupid' can be used in either a humorous or mean-spirited way. The context will determine how the word is perceived.

The context behind Lucky Girl Syndrome is simply this:

To help you harness the power of luck and the principles behind it so that you can transform your life from a series of random events into a deliberate adventure of opportunity, growth, and fulfilment.

Regardless of what you currently think of Lucky Girl Syndrome, there is inherently no malice behind it – watch any video on the topic, and yes, it may annoy you to hear a high-pitched person banging on about sh*t you just don't care about, but it all stems from a good place.

Cynically speaking, the term Lucky Girl Syndrome was probably created for shock value. Regarding only the psychological basis and disregarding the name, people will (hopefully) stop being so offended by it.

One of my favourite words is 'terracotta'. When I say it, I automatically picture a big olive tree in a terracotta pot in Spain. That is a positive perception.

What if one day someone decided that the word 'terracotta' had negative connotations and influenced people to see it as a catchy swear word? It would eventually be used as an insult to emphasise negative things. The actual *word* doesn't mean anything. It's the negative association people give words that makes them negative. So if we all decided to keep saying 'terracotta' all the time, people would stop caring. The shock value would subside, and it would become another word again.

We're undermining a system flawed through the overuse of words that are made out to be harmful, when in fact they are just letters, mixed together like every other word. Now we know that Lucky Girl Syndrome is not strictly for 'girls' nor is it a 'syndrome' and there is no ill intention behind it, let's move beyond what we *think* it is and get down to business of discovering what it's all about. And no, we're not going to change the name nor the title of this book (besides, it's clearly gone to print).

The Latest Trendy Trend

Social media has not only revolutionised how we interact and share information, but it has also significantly impacted various aspects of our lives. Whether you are wise to the cruxes of social media or not, and whether you like to admit it or not, at some point in our lives, social media has had a major influence on our ideations, opinions, style, trends, where we take our next vacation, our views on politics, and even the way we approach manifestation.

Social media has propelled the widespread acceptance and utilisation of manifestation techniques, and Lucky Girl Syndrome has snowballed on social media platforms, transforming manifestation techniques into a viral phenomenon.

Why? . . .

- **Powerful Influence of Social Media:** Social media platforms are powerful influencers, shaping public opinions and dictating the trends and ideas that go viral. These platforms enable users to access a vast range of information and engage with diverse communities. As manifestation techniques gained popularity on social media, individuals were increasingly exposed to success stories, testimonials, and techniques that purportedly facilitated the attainment of their desires.

- **Accessibility and Democratisation of Information:** Social media's accessibility has made manifestation techniques more inclusive and readily available to individuals globally. Previously, such information was confined to books or select communities. Now, people can access these techniques effortlessly, irrespective of their geographical location or socio-economic background. This democratisation of knowledge empowers individuals by providing them with the tools to manifest their aspirations.

- **Community Building and Collective Empowerment:** Social media promotes the formation of online communities centred around manifestation techniques, providing a space for like-minded individuals to share experiences, exchange ideas, and support each other's endeavours. This sharing of success stories and manifestations creates a sense of collective community, reinforcing beliefs in the effectiveness of these techniques. This camaraderie further fuels the viral nature of manifestation techniques, as we encourage and inspire one another.

- **The Role of Visual Content and Confirmation Bias:** Social media's visual nature facilitates the spread of manifestation techniques, incorporating images and videos making the practices more relatable and compelling. Visual representations of desired outcomes strengthen the belief that manifestation techniques work, leading us to feel more inclined to engage with these practices.

- **Confirmation Bias:** People tend to gravitate towards evidence that aligns with their beliefs, seeking confirmation of the effectiveness of these techniques. As social media platforms amplify success stories and positive manifestations, people are more likely to embrace and share these techniques, perpetuating the cycle of virality.

- **Escapism and Hope:** In an uncertain climate, manifestation techniques offer us a sense of control and hope. Social media platforms often act as an escape and provide possibilities. The idea that one can manifest their desires and achieve 'lucky girl' status creates a captivating narrative, making it all the more appealing in an era of constant change and unpredictability.

Lucky Girl Syndrome has successfully embraced these social media capabilities, carving out a widespread trend and amplifying its message. The concept has gained viral popularity due to:

- **Catchy Content:** The hashtag #LuckyGirlSyndrome has been used over 400 million times on TikTok, most videos associated with the hashtag are short, catchy, and visually appealing, making them easy to share and watch, thus helping to spread the trend quickly.

- **Powerful Positivity:** This message is appealing, especially on social media, where positive thinking and self-affirmation are often celebrated.

- **Influencer Involvement:** Several popular TikTok influencers have promoted Lucky Girl Syndrome, boosting credibility and attracting their highly engaged audiences to amplify the trend.

A trend that will grow and then die a slow death until the next manifestation technique appears? Or could there be a longer-term line of thought here?

The accessibility to harness the trend, the sense of community and empowerment it fosters, the visual content utilised, and the hope and escapism it offers, all contribute to LGS's virality.

A Lucky Life

When we don't appreciate what we have, we may develop the false belief that everything is easy, and we are just lucky to have everything in our lives.

To an extent, this type of mindset is lovely and comforting, perhaps even trying to protect us, but it encourages any belief that everything is handed to you on a silver platter and that you don't have to work hard for the good in your life.

Thinking that you don't need work ethic, dedication, and persistence to get lucky not only causes a sense of entitlement but will also require medical intervention to help surgically remove your head out of your arse, which will almost certainly limit luck in your life.

Achieving luck requires dedication, persistence, and substantial hard work. Those who work diligently and persevere are more likely to achieve their goals than those who solely wait for Lady Luck to work in their favour.

The misconception that success solely derives from luck is fallacious. The lucky ones often possess qualities like perseverance, determination, and informed decision-making. While luck certainly aids success, it's not the sole determinant. Psychologist Angela Duckworth introduced the concept of 'grit', which refers to a combination of passion and perseverance for long-term goals. In her pioneering research, Duckworth found that individuals with higher levels of 'grit' were more likely to achieve their goals, even when faced with challenges and setbacks, suggesting that perseverance and determination are needed for success.[1] Carol Dweck's research also dissects the notion of mindset – those with a 'fixed mindset' believe their abilities are innate and unchangeable, and those with an 'incremental mindset' believe in the power of effort and growth. People with an incremental mindset are more likely to persevere, seek challenges, and embrace learning opportunities, leading to greater achievement.[2]

Adopt an incremental mindset alongside your view of success, and start to see luck and hard work as mutually exclusive.

In job applications, for instance, luck might secure interviews, but hard work is vital to proving suitability. Luck opens doors, and diligent effort capitalises on opportunities. They complement each other, amplifying the likelihood of success.

Luck and hard work aren't polar opposites; they form two sides of the same coin. Luck can give you opportunities, but it is up to you to work hard and take advantage of those opportunities. If you are lucky and work hard, you will achieve success.

To lead a lucky life, work with your core values when it comes to attracting and creating opportunities. By aligning your actions and decisions with what truly matters to you, you emit positive energy that attracts favourable circumstances. Trusting in your core values allows you to make choices that are authentic and in line with your true self, increasing the likelihood of attracting luck and opening doors to new possibilities.

The Debrief: Discovering Your Core Values

- **Reflect:** Think about moments in your life when you felt most fulfilled. These can be big accomplishments or small ones. What made them so meaningful?

- **Identify:** Identify the emotions you experienced during those times. Were you feeling empowered, joyful, connected, challenged, or something else?

- **List What Matters:** Make a list of aspects of your life that you deeply care about. These could be related to relationships, career, personal growth, community, health, spirituality, creativity – anything!

- **Prioritise:** Review and rank them in order of importance. What matters the most to you?

What would you prioritise, even if it meant sacrificing something else?

- **Find Common Themes:** Look for common themes or values that emerge. For example, if 'helping others' and 'personal growth' are prominent, your core values might include compassion and self-improvement.

- **Reflect:** Take a moment to reflect on your emerging core values. Do they resonate with you? Do they align with the moments when you felt truly fulfilled? If they do, you're likely on the right track.

- **Finalise:** Based on your reflections, distil your list down to a few key core values that resonate deeply with you. These values should guide your decisions, actions, and priorities.

- **Integrate:** Identifying your core values, consider integrating them into your daily life. How can you make choices that align with these values? How can they influence your relationships, goals, and pursuits?

- **Rinse & Repeat:** Core values can evolve. Make a habit to regularly reflect and reassess your values as you grow and experience new phases of life.

(continued)

(*continued*)

Focusing on holistic desires allows you to align your manifestations with your core values and beliefs.

My core values are: _____

_____

Thoughts and Reflections

Whatever objections, judgements, or limiting thoughts you may have surrounding luck or manifesting – simply being open at this stage is key.

This chapter is a basic introduction to give you an idea of Lucky Girl. Luck is not solely dependent on genetics, fate, or chance but is a combination of factors such as mindset, effort, and strategy. This book will help you establish a more comprehensive perspective, explore components of luck, shed light on its causes and effects. Throughout the following pages, you will start to create your Lucky narrative, identify areas where you may be going wrong, and re-evaluate to get back on the path of attracting true luck.

Remember, LGS is not waving a magic wand that will guarantee that good things will happen to you all the time. You will not get everything you want just by thinking about it. Sorry – a Lamborghini isn't going to turn up on your driveway tomorrow just because you popped it on your vision board before bed (*unless you have a generous sugar daddy, so more fool him!*). You will, however, should you put in the required effort, hard work, persistence, and appreciation, attract what you desire.

LGS is another *spicy* ingredient to get you there – where you can focus on the positive and create an environment where good things are encouraged.

Recognising this now will help you in the long run.

We can't control outcomes in life, even with all the luck in the world. We can, however, control our *responses* to it.

Soon you will start to see that with a little bit of luck and a whole load of hard work, you can achieve your dreams – *I promise*.

So prepare to get uncomfortable, move away from misconceptions, open your hearts and minds, and, as RuPaul so beautifully puts it, 'You better work, bitch!'

Take a breath, and let's begin . . .

2

The Bullshit and the Balance

Nowadays, wherever you go, whatever you choose to do or not do, however you appear, or whatever you post online, someone will doubtless be criticising you – or at least certainly have an opinion.

Criticism is a funny thing, and not all of it is bad. In the media, it can serve two purposes: to help consumers make informed decisions about what to buy or watch; or to help hold businesses and organisations accountable for their actions. Additionally, criticism can spark debate and discussion about important issues.

Social media was once heralded as a platform for connecting people and a hub for sharing diverse content, including positive messages and self-improvement strategies. However, despite the abundance of uplifting content, sadly, people are becoming increasingly toxic and critical of such positivity, and we are witnessing a worrisome surge in criticism. From heated political debates to harsh judgements on personal posts, the digital landscape has become progressively polarised.

A key factor contributing to the rise of criticism on social media is the formation of echo chambers. Social media algorithms often show content based on users' preferences, reinforcing their existing beliefs and ideologies. As a result, people encounter like-minded views, intensifying their convictions and fostering more criticism of opposing perspectives.

The cloak of anonymity provided by social media allows us to express ourselves without immediate consequences. This can lead to the 'online disinhibition effect', where people are more likely to engage in harsh criticism, cyberbullying, and trolling. The lack of face-to-face accountability has amplified negativity on social media platforms.

In the competitive attention economy, media outlets and users may resort to clickbait headlines and sensational content to grab viewers' attention. This quest for clicks and engagement often leads to the spread of controversial and provocative content, which fuels criticism and negativity.

Social and political polarisation have spilled over into the digital realm, contributing to the rise of divisive discourse on social media. As people gravitate towards like-minded communities, they become more entrenched in their beliefs and less tolerant of opposing viewpoints, leading to heightened criticism and negativity.

Platforms are susceptible to emotional contagion, where strong emotions spread rapidly through posts, comments, and shares. Viral outrage can fuel a mob mentality, encouraging users to participate in criticism and negative exchanges without fully understanding the context or consequences.

For society, the polarisation and negativity on social media can deepen existing divisions and hinder productive dialogue on critical issues. The spread of misinformation and hostile exchanges can erode trust in institutions and weaken social cohesion.

This increasing rise in negativity on social media is creating quite a hostile environment. In this space, it deters people from expressing themselves authentically and engaging in open, constructive discussions. It dims our light and makes us hold back. We feel suppressed. We feel it now more than ever – it's becoming easier to say nothing than be honest with our opinions and share how we truly feel.

But why, if behind Lucky Girl Syndrome there is nothing but an underlying positive message, are people hating on it so much?

Primarily, it's because of the reasons just stated. Strong opinions and the critical nature of the discourse around Lucky Girl Syndrome stem from a combination of emotional engagement, sensationalism, confirmation bias, anonymity, competition, and societal divides. As social media continues to evolve, understanding these factors can help foster more constructive and informed discussions that promote dialogue and mutual understanding.

Flipping to another side – perhaps there is actual good reasoning behind the criticism of Lucky Girl Syndrome? Perhaps *it really is* full of bullshit?

Lucky Girl doesn't give itself a good rep due to its association with commercialism, celebrity culture, and new-age spirituality. And since growing in virality, publications and journalists have been tearing apart LGS, with *The Guardian* writing, 'it isn't anything new and has a dark side', and *Forbes* giving people 'tips to recover from Lucky Girl Syndrome'.

Oh and let's not forget the trolls . . . Upon researching LGS, I went from fits of giggles to being utterly horrified at the comments behind some posts on LGS TikToks.

The TikTok star, Laura Galebe, who brought Lucky Girl Syndrome to life, conducted a study, and found that women who subscribed to LGS were more likely to engage in magical thinking and to have unrealistic expectations about their lives. Additionally, a study by Richard Wiseman found that people who believed they were lucky were more likely to attribute their successes to luck and their failures to other factors.

Engaging in a self-conducted investigation, I distributed a questionnaire on Instagram to root around the sentiments surrounding Lucky Girl Syndrome. However, the results yielded a diverse array of opinions, ranging from positive to negative:

Positive sentiments:

- 'I think LGS can be a positive force, helping people to stay positive and optimistic.'

- 'I believe that everyone has some degree of luck and that it's important to be grateful for the good things that happen to us.'

- 'I think LGS can help people to take risks and to try new things.'

- 'I quite like the idea of looking for luck in my life.'

Negative sentiments:

- 'I think LGS can be a harmful belief that can lead to entitlement and unrealistic expectations.'

- 'I believe that luck is not the only factor that determines success, and that hard work and determination are also important.'

- 'I think LGS can lead people to believe that they are immune to misfortune, which can be dangerous.'

- 'What the f*ck is Lucky Girl Syndrome?'

Overall, the sentiment behind Lucky Girl Syndrome is mixed. There is evidence to suggest that LGS can be both harmful and beneficial. The points outlined in this chapter are key so that you can be fully aware of the potential risks and benefits of Lucky Girl Syndrome before subscribing to this belief.

When analysing the actual content of #LuckyGirlSyndrome, a lot of the messaging was totally missing the mark and not fully grasping the concept of luck, which is influencing and misleading audiences, steering them in the wrong direction . . . and yes, this type of content does encourage that sense of entitlement and ultimately adheres to the narrative of toxic positivity, which makes luck seem like a fad . . . and that is bullshit.

Like with anything in life, there is a balance. We should be encouraging others to live a life beyond their wildest dreams and to be real. We're going to look into the BS behind LGS, but we're also giving some guidance on how to create that overall blissful balance.

Moaning about Manifestation

The idea of manifestation has been around for centuries, making the theory behind Lucky Girl Syndrome nothing overly revolutionary, but it is a shiny new face in the body of the Law of Attraction. The whole notion, of course, has its sceptics. I myself, at times, have been one of them. Sceptics are people who approach new ideas with caution and often require evidence before accepting them as true. Really – we're all sceptics at heart.

We are critical thinkers who rely on empirical evidence and are hesitant to embrace concepts that cannot be verified; therefore, when it comes to the Law of Attraction or Lucky Girl Syndrome, sceptics find it hard to accept that the mere power of thought can attract success and happiness.

They argue it's nothing more than a pseudoscientific concept that has no real evidence to back it up. I mean, how can you actually measure something like this?

A critic's job is to – guess what – be critical.

There are around 8 billion people on planet Earth (and counting), and a huge majority of them pan the notion of manifestation. The fact that it promotes a belief in a 'magical' or 'mystical' force that is lacking in science is one of the primary reasons. Common techniques of manifestation, à la Lucky Girl Syndrome, lack empirical evidence to support their effectiveness. In fact, some studies have shown that excessive positive thinking can actually hinder performance and lead to unrealistic expectations.

No Scientific Evidence

New-age spirituality is controversial due to its lack of empirical evidence and scientific limitations. Critics argue it oversimplifies social issues and is associated with commercialism. Evaluating claims and seeking alternative explanations is crucial. Thousands worldwide claim manifestation success through the Law of Attraction (LOA) but verifying and generalising these claims is challenging. The method's vague framing makes scientific testing difficult. Manifestation techniques attribute outcomes to unobservable forces, hindering objective observation and measurement.

There have even been studies that have attempted to test the manifestation, all of which produced mixed and inconclusive results. A 2006 research review by psychologists Michael Shermer and David N. Menton concluded that there is 'no scientific evidence that the law of attraction works'.[1] A 2010 study by French psychologist Eric Gressier found no significance between visualisation and performance in a motor coordination task.[2] Similarly, a 2016 study by British psychologists found no evidence that the LOA improves academic or creative performance.[3] These studies suggest that the Law of Attraction is not a reliable or predictable phenomenon that can be replicated or applied universally.

Can we seriously argue with science?

Manifestation methods draw criticism for oversimplifying complex phenomena. The Law of Attraction simplifies outcomes to thoughts and emotions, disregarding external factors like social structures and history. Critics say LOA blames individuals and ignores systemic problems like poverty and discrimination.

Science does prove that life is all about *balance*.

Lucky Girl Syndrome comes with its warnings, and striking that important balance between being a lucky soul and not an absolute arse is imperative here. Despite the BS, negative press, and oh-so-many opinions surrounding the topic, Lucky Girl Syndrome *can* and *does* create miracles. You can wish whatever you want and manifest to your heart's content, but you need to be aware of the surrounding BS, find a balance, and create a strong strategy and clear roadmap of the actions to take to attract.

Let's pop on our critical thinking caps; class is in session.

The following sections explain why Lucky Girl Syndrome is bullshit and provide alternative ways to understand each objection, weighing up both sides of the argument.

We Can't Ignore Our Current Realities

Lucy Girl Syndrome can overlook reality by focusing solely on positive aspects while disregarding challenges. For instance, in financial struggles, you emphasise having a roof over your head but ignore pay cheque to pay cheque living. LGS doesn't shield from misfortune, so don't be led to impulsive actions and a belief that hard work is unnecessary.

Additionally, sceptics argue that the Lucky Girl technique is too simplistic and does not take into account the complexity of real-life situations. It suggests that thoughts will bring about financial success, when various factors such as education, family background, and the state of the economy have a more significant impact on one's overall finances.

Ignoring your current reality can have far-reaching negative effects on various aspects of your life. It's ignorant and selfish to deny it.

Strike the Balance: Get Real

We should all have goals and hopes for the future and plans that we would like to fulfil. Without getting to grips with what's realistic and what isn't and learning the guiding principles (all of which you will learn in this book!) you're setting yourself up for disappointment and unmanageable expectations.

As much as I'd like to 'Lucky Girl' myself into winning the EuroMillions lottery tonight (and yes, I've bought a ticket because someone has to win!), we do have to be realistic here. It would be fantastic if I won £50, let alone £5 million. Statistically speaking, you are heartbreakingly more likely to get hit by lightning on your way to purchase your ticket, than winning – the odds of winning the UK's EuroMillions are one in 139.8 million and according to *National Geographic*, the odds of being struck in your lifetime are 1 in 3,000. *Great.*

You shouldn't be put off from buying your ticket because of that statistic, but you probably shouldn't be quitting your job in the hopes you do, and you definitely shouldn't be buying a ticket over sacrificing eating that night.

Expecting luck to just happen and relying solely on it without preparing for potential obstacles can give you unrealistic expectations, so strike a balance by acknowledging the reality of your current circumstances. By facing reality with honesty and courage, you set yourself on a path towards greater self-awareness and develop a healthier mindset.

As I said, someone has to win the lottery – so don't be discouraged from buying your ticket, but equally, don't be heartbroken if those balls don't pull out your magic numbers tonight!

Don't undermine your reality – Lucky Girl is a valuable tool to help you achieve success and should be complemented with a realistic mindset and achievable milestones.

It's Impossible to Be Positive All the Time

Wait – there is seriously a downside to being *too* positive?

To be a Lucky Girl, or use any technique of manifestation for that matter, of course, you're going to have to work on the principles of positive thinking. However, if you go into manifestation blindly, believing that you constantly need to sustain positivity all the time in order to attract, this will be your pitfall.

Unless you're a Tibetan zen monk living in the Himalayas, I think you'll really struggle with staying positive *all* the freaking time.

The world isn't always positive; it's beautiful yet includes challenges. Life has ups and downs, and all our various emotions are natural. Maintaining constant positivity during tough times is just too much!

Say someone bumps into the back of your car – you're safe, but there's a dent on your bumper, and your neck is already a little sore.

Manifestation experts will say at that very moment you should be thinking how lucky you are to be alive (that can come later, once you've calmed your nervous system), but are we seriously expecting that to be our intrinsic natural reaction? Hell no. In that very moment a natural reaction and emotion is, for most, shock. So it's OK to think, 'Oh my gosh my neck hurts!' and 'Great, now I have to get my car fixed on top of everything else' or 'What a f*cking arsehole that person is to run into me'.

Our emotions are dynamic and responsive to the ever-changing circumstances of life. Emotions such as happiness, sadness, fear, and anger serve as adaptive functions (helping us navigate challenges and opportunities) and guide us through challenges and the highs and lows we encounter every day. Attempting to remain positive all the time denies the natural ebb and flow of emotions, potentially leading to emotional suppression and denial, which can be detrimental to mental well-being.

Evolution has wired human brains with a negativity bias, meaning we are more attuned to negative stimuli and experiences for survival purposes. This inherent bias ensures that we stay vigilant to potential threats in our environment. Positivity has its place, but the negativity bias navigates potential risks and dangers appropriately.

Maintaining positivity requires significant cognitive resources, and our brains have a limited capacity for processing emotions and information. As a result, attempting to suppress or avoid negative emotions to focus on positivity can lead to cognitive overload and emotional exhaustion.

To really attract luck into your life you must be genuine and authentic, especially when it comes to positivity. They say a fake smile can lead to a real one, and there's evidence to suggest so, but if you're seriously hurting inside and struggling and going out into the world with a brave, happy, smiling face, you are doing yourself a huge injustice by not honouring how you truly feel, which is more emotionally damaging in the long run as you are not exploring your underlying emotional issues.

Psychologists have also shown that relying solely on positive thinking can be counterproductive. A study published in the *Journal of Personality and Social Psychology* found that participants who only focused on positive emotions were less likely to achieve their goals.[4] This is because negative emotions can provide us with valuable feedback and help us make necessary adjustments to our behaviour.

A rule in manifestation is that you need to keep an unwavering faith of positivity all the time, even when it's impossible . . . and that's bullshit. It's exhausting!

We're indeed going to have to adapt to a certain degree of positivity, to emit vibrational frequency and optimism – I repeat, it's about being **realistic.**

Positivity has its benefits; however, the science of human emotions and psychology highlights that it is unrealistic to maintain it constantly. Emotions are dynamic, and accepting the full range of feelings is vital to attracting what you want. Going in blindly to Lucky Girl Syndrome, thinking it's all about staying super positive all the time, will exhaust you and work against your desires. Don't create more hard work for yourself – give it a rest.

Strike the Balance: Be Positive, Without Being Too Positive

You heard.

Apologies if this is getting confusing here – aside from giving it a rest on the positive front, you're going to have to keep a degree of positivity in your tank. Don't be so positive that you're sounding like Ross in the tv show *Friends* when he says 'I'M FINE' when learning about his ex, Rachel, dating his beloved best pal Joey; or like the meme of the dog sitting in a room on fire. And don't be a negative Nancy either – create a balance where you are you, just with an *optimistic outlook*.

Let's discuss the psychology of attribution.

This refers to how individuals interpret and explain the causes of events, outcomes, and behaviours in their lives. People often make attributions either positively or negatively, depending on their beliefs, personality traits, and past experiences. In the context of manifestation, understanding the implications of positive and negative attribution is vital in nurturing a mindset that supports the achievement of goals.

Positive Attribution

This entails linking success to internal, stable, and controllable factors. A positive attribution style views achievements as a product of effort, skills, and persistence. This mindset empowers individuals to proactively pursue their goals.

Bernard Weiner's research showed that positive attributions for success boost self-esteem and motivation. This self-efficacy enhances belief in achieving goals, making positive attribution valuable for manifestation.[5] Albert Bandura emphasised positive self-attribution's role in building self-efficacy and resilience and found acknowledging efforts promotes proactive behaviours, persistence, and goal attainment.[6]

Negative Attribution

On the other hand, negative attribution involves attributing success to external, unstable, and uncontrollable factors. Individuals with a negative attribution style may dismiss their accomplishments as mere luck or believe that external circumstances played a dominant role in their achievements.

Research by Semmel et al. found that consistently making negative attributions increases the risk of learned helplessness, reduces belief in personal agency, and blocks manifestation progress.[7] In a review exploring optimism and mental health, psychologists showed that a positive attribution style works well with manifestation principles, leading to goal attainment, persistence, hope and optimism.[8]

When it comes to manifestation, adopting a positive attribution style is generally more advantageous, as the belief is that personal efforts and intentions help achieve desired outcomes and produce a proactive and determined mindset. Positive attributions empower us to take responsibility for our actions and make the necessary efforts to manifest luck.

A positive attribution style is not about being positive all the time. Indeed, it is a cognitive process that shapes how you perceive the causes of events and influences your emotional reactions and behaviour. Adopting this style when faced with both positive and negative experiences doesn't suppress your emotions, works with personal agency, and helps you take proactive steps and refocus your intentions.

Acting like you're always on an acid trip, away with the fairies in positivity land vs being a grumpy, pessimistic, miserable donkey like Eeyore from *Winnie the Pooh* are two opposite ends of the spectrum, and we don't want either. Find your feet with a positive attributional style and step into a more realistic, optimistic version of yourself.

Thinking you have to be nothing but a positive princess all the time is the flaw of Lucky Girl Syndrome. However, in order to create our balance, we must learn to remain optimistic and adopt a positive attribution style. Consider yourself lucky each and every day, approach life with confidence and control, but also commit to learning other routes to your desired future, aside from positive thinking – which you'll learn throughout this book.

Being Delusional Actually Works against You

It's no wonder that since growing in virality, critics have panned this idea of Lucky Girls with creators encouraging their audiences to 'BE DELUSIONAL'.

To grab attention, soundbites such as 'be delusional' are often used – the underlying message behind the phrase is to inspire positive thinking and confidence, which is helpful to an extent, but it can be quite problematic in that it is an extreme version of visualisation.

The term 'delusional' carries a negative connotation due to its association with irrational and distorted thinking that deviates from reality. It signifies a detachment from commonly accepted truths, often lacking logical basis. In the context of mental health, it's linked to conditions like schizophrenia, implying mental instability. Describing someone as delusional suggests their perceptions are inaccurate and don't coincide with social norms, contributing to its negative implications. While a clinical term, it's important to use language that respects diverse viewpoints when discussing beliefs or opinions outside of a clinical context.

The idea behind using the term 'be delusional' when it comes to manifesting is to encourage people to believe that they can achieve or attract anything they want.

Delusion is a mental state in which a person holds beliefs that are not shared by others or that are not based on reality. This can lead to problems in a person's life, such as difficulty functioning in society, making decisions, and forming relationships.

When it comes to Lucky Girl Syndrome and manifesting, delusion can lead people to believe that they are immune to misfortune or that they deserve good things simply because they believe they are lucky. When you live in a state of delulu, detrimental impact on your mental health, the pressure to manifest outcomes without considering the realities of life and living with delusions, can lead to increased stress, anxiety, and feelings of inadequacy when desired results are not achieved or when things don't go your way. Additionally, it can lead people to avoid taking risks or challenging themselves, as they may be afraid that if they do, they will lose their luck.

Don't set yourself up for disappointment here. Delusion can also lead to confirmation bias. Meaning that when you believe you are lucky, you may start to interpret events in your life in a way that confirms your belief. For example, if you believe you are lucky because of your promotion at work, you may interpret this as a sign that you are, indeed, lucky. However, say the promotion gets passed to your rival co-worker instead, you may interpret this as a sign that you are not as lucky as you thought, rather than a temporary setback.

Strike the Balance: Daydream

Say you see a piece of content online that says, *Be delusional. The money is coming.*

That does not mean we should start racking up bills on a credit card to pay later and take ourselves on a luxury shopping spree because we think 'the money's coming' – NO!

Lucky Girl Syndrome is not about bankrupting yourself.

Those who encourage 'be delusional' have a responsibility to provide proper context and guidance. Without it, their audience (especially the younger generation) may internalise these messages without understanding the nuances of goal-setting and manifestation.

If you are considering the 'be delusional' approach to Lucky Girl Syndrome and manifesting, be aware of these potential dangers and take steps to protect yourself. Again, this includes being realistic about your goals and expectations and balancing with your optimistic outlook.

Don't fall into the trap of delusion because it will only overwhelm, confuse, and block your manifestations.

The antidote to delusion is to daydream. Create equilibrium by daydreaming, and visualise your way to success in a healthier manner.

Visualisation is a potent manifestation technique that involves mentally imagining and experiencing one's desired outcomes and is referenced a lot in the manifestation world. It's said to enhance focus and motivation but must be balanced with actionable steps toward achieving those goals.

One popular study involved a group of people who were asked to visualise themselves being successful in achieving their goals. The study found that those who regularly visualise themselves 'succeeding' were more likely to achieve their goals than those who did not.

Daydreaming about how we want our future to look, or what some call visualisation, is totally normal and a healthy thing to do.

The phrase 'be delusional' is argued to be a helpful approach to challenging your limiting beliefs, but it's perpetuating a false narrative. Instead, allow your daydreams to take you beyond your limitations, by aligning them with your thoughts and desired outcomes. Immerse yourself in any belief that your dreams are within your reach, and allow your daydreams help you choose your next actionable step.

In that respect, surely, we can all benefit from tapping into our imagination once in a while!

Lucky Girl vs Lazy Girl

One of the arguments against Lucky Girl Syndrome (LGS) is the assumption that people who believe in it place too much emphasis on positive thinking, thus neglecting real-world action and necessary work.

It's true – most of the videos on the topic talk purely of manifesting through thinking and leave out many important ingredients, like action.

Relying on LGS can lead to laziness and a mindset of passivity, focusing on external factors rather than personal effort. This mindset can result in complacency, lack of motivation, and reduced productivity. For example, consider a student who relies solely on LGS to pass an important exam. If the student believes that luck will somehow favour them, they may not invest the necessary time and effort studying diligently and preparing thoroughly, thinking that LGS will carry them through. This attitude can lead to poor performance on the exam and potentially halt their academic progress.

Likewise, in professional endeavours – imagine an employee who believes that promotions and career advancements are solely a matter of luck, without considering the need to develop new skills, contribute to the team, or take on additional responsibilities. This mindset can prevent the employee from seeking opportunities for growth, further education, or skills. As a result, they might miss out on chances for advancement and career success due to their complacency and lack of proactive effort.

Strike the Balance: Take Aligned Action

Relying on luck creates a passive mindset that discourages action. To avoid this trap, be enlightened to form a mindset of personal responsibility and action. Believe in luck but believe in yourself to create it through hard work.

Your proactive approach propels you to consistently work towards your desires. Consequently, you identify and seize opportunities due to active engagement and a mindset attuned to potential success paths. The universe responds to this proactive energy by presenting unforeseen chances for growth and success.

It's all about taking aligned action. Aligned action refers to taking purposeful steps and making decisions in harmony with your true self, your values, and your goals. It's about living intentionally and moving forward in a way that resonates with your core beliefs and aspirations.

When you take aligned action, you're not just going through the motions; you're moving with a sense of purpose and conviction.

In this pursuit of personal and professional success, never underestimate the profound impact of taking action. Jack Canfield's book *The Success Principles: How to Get from Where You Are to Where You Want to Be* (a highly recommended Lucky Girl read!), serves as a guiding light, emphasising the vital role of proactive steps in achieving one's goals.

Canfield's book underlines the foundational principle of taking 100% responsibility for one's life, and through this concept, you recognise that it is you who holds the power to shape your circumstances, and that initiation all starts with the process of taking action. The act of translating dreams and goals into tangible steps is not merely an option but a necessity. When you commit to working to execute your aspirations you seize control of your destiny, ushering in a transformational adventure.

There is no overnight miracle; you've got to do the work, Lucky Girl!

Lights, camera, **action.**

Don't Be Encouraged by Entitlement

Critics and numerous articles assert that the application of Lucky Girl Syndrome often portrays individuals effortlessly receiving rewards, potentially promoting entitlement. This dynamic can fuel the perception that manifestation leads to feelings of entitlement and inflated self-importance, attributing positive outcomes solely to luck rather than effort. Entitlement involves expecting special treatment or privileges without earning them, often linked to a sense of superiority. This mindset can be detrimental, causing unrealistic expectations, impaired decision-making, and interpersonal conflicts.

Upon analysing the hashtag #luckygirlsyndrome you probably find your eyes rolling. Entitlement does shine through, and that's something we can all probably agree on.

Strike the Balance: Get Your Head Out of Your Arse

Rather than leaning towards entitlement, be encouraged to take responsibility for your life, actively work towards getting what it is you want, and overall, get your head out of your arse. Ensure whatever beliefs you have do not become an excuse for inaction or a sense of entitlement, but rather a springboard into your life's right direction. Or perhaps helping others in the process.

To combat the detrimental effects of Lucky Girl Syndrome, you must embrace self-awareness and positive self-attribution.

Soon you will be doing just that – recognising your capabilities and empowering your efforts, so you can go about life, challenge yourself and your goals, persist through adversity, and achieve genuine success. By promoting a culture that celebrates merit and competence over entitlement, you will nurture genuine confidence and personal growth.

Women Are Not Luckier than Men

Why is it that women who have achieved success in their careers or personal lives are often viewed as 'blessed', 'fortunate', or 'lucky'?

The myth that women are luckier than men is inaccurate and harmful, as it undermines the hard work, dedication, and sacrifices women have made to achieve success in their careers and personal lives. Let's debunk this misconception; it perpetuates gender inequality by denying women proper recognition and opportunities. Women face numerous challenges in society, including lower pay, violence, and less representation in power positions. Gender stereotypes often associate women with communal traits rather than leadership or competence, undermining their self-efficacy and perpetuating the belief that their achievements are a result of luck. This perception of Lucky Girl stems from deeply ingrained societal expectations and norms that perpetuate the idea that women's accomplishments are merely serendipitous occurrences rather than the culmination of hard work and dedication. This notion can manifest in various ways, such as a successful female entrepreneur being brushed off as lucky for securing investors or a talented actress being seen as fortunate for a coveted role.

We don't need another history lesson reminding us how women have been confined to certain roles, but we must never forget the discrimination in various spheres that has contributed to the reinforcement of these stereotypes.

The perception of Lucky Girl can harm those striving to achieve similar heights, as they may internalise the idea that success is more about being in the right place at the right time than working diligently towards their goals. This can lead to a lack of self-confidence and deter them from pursuing ambitious endeavours, perpetuating a cycle of inequality and missed opportunities.

Strike the Balance: Promote Equality

To combat this syndrome, society must actively challenge and redefine conventional notions of femininity and success. It's essential to acknowledge the barriers and biases women face while navigating their paths to success and to dismantle the societal expectations that trivialise their achievements. Celebrating the hard work and dedication of accomplished women can inspire future generations to pursue their dreams with confidence and resilience, knowing that success is attainable through their efforts and determination.

By promoting diverse narratives, we can shift the prevailing perception from one of mere luck to one that highlights the immense strength, resilience, and determination that lie at the core of anyone's accomplishments. Only then can we create a more equitable and supportive society where every person's achievements are celebrated as the result of their own perseverance and tenacity rather than perceived as the product of chance.

Manifestation Is So Much More than Materialism

Analysing LGS content, an overwhelming narrative is about manifesting materialistic things.

I'm sure the majority of us would love to be able to own a mortgage-free mansion by the sea, with a sports car on the drive and all the money in the world to not care about how much it costs to fill up with petrol, and a walk-in closet filled with the latest designer clothes – we don't have to deny that BUT this is exactly where LGS is fundamentally is getting it wrong.

For modern day humans, we are constantly striving to find happiness and often mistake it for thinking it's in something we can either purchase or acquire.

Materialism isn't a new phenomenon – even in the Stone Age, cavemen and women valued certain possessions they believed were important for their survival. Albeit not the same idea of materialism we have today, but the point is that it's something that's been around for a very long time, and is ingrained in society.

Why we love the shiny new toy:

- Sign of success – associated with wealth, power, and status. As a result, people tend to look to manifestation to attract materialistic things in order to feel that sense of success.

- Security – materialistic objects can give a sense of control and comfort.

- Impress others – psychology suggests that when we attain material things, we see it as making a good impression.

While tangible goods provide comfort and convenience, focusing solely on material things during the manifestation process can have its consequences.

Material possessions do bring feelings of happiness and satisfaction. I remember so badly wanting a Furby that my dad queued in the snow for four hours to get one. To this day I still remember the enormous amount of joy I felt unwrapping it out of the box and its freaky eyes opening. I loved that Furby until the day its batteries went. Like the Furby's batteries, that pleasure was short-lived. As the excitement derived from new acquisitions tends to fade quickly, placing too much emphasis on material things can create a never-ending cycle of consumption and a need to chase the next item we believe can bring fulfilment. Worse, you may find yourself unsatisfied even when you do achieve your material goals because you have neglected to address your deeper, more meaningful desires.

When our personal value is tied solely to material possessions, we risk defining ourselves by what we own rather than who we are as human beings. If we become too fixated on material goods, it diverts our attention away from our personal development and emotional well-being.

Life is much more than physical possessions. Love, relationships, health, and happiness – these are all things that cannot be bought or possessed, but are essential for a fulfilling life, essential to being a Lucky Girl. When we focus on those things that matter most, we will find that we are, actually, less interested in materialistic things. We will also find that we become more content and happier with our lives – and once you get to this satisfying place, should it be that you do then quite fancy a dazzling brand new, state-of-the-art ***insert your materialistic desire***, then you are, for sure, more likely to attract it and bring it into your reality.

Strike the Balance: Manifest Wisely

For those utilising Lucky Girl to attract material possessions, that's absolutely OK, but first, delve into the underlying motives. Ask yourself if you're seeking success, security, validation from others, personal growth, finding a soulmate, enhancing relationships, or making a meaningful impact on the world. If you have been preoccupied with materialistic desires and ignored your genuine needs and aspirations, that's OK too. Read on – throughout this book, you will explore the dimensions of emotions, spirituality, and social connections in your life. This exploration forms a compass that leads you towards authenticity and purpose. This introspection guides you towards aligning your goals with your core values and true desires and starting to shape your Lucky Girl narrative.

It's Playing a Role in the Privilege Problem

Critics will argue that manifestation can perpetuate a culture of victim-blaming and privilege. The idea that one can manifest whatever they desire could lead to the belief that those who are struggling financially or facing other challenges simply aren't manifesting hard enough or correctly. Lucky Girl Syndrome tends to overlook the structural barriers and discriminatory practices that prevent equal opportunities for everyone. It places the onus of success solely on individual qualities, disregarding the impact of institutionalised prejudices and unequal access to education, healthcare, and economic factors that many face.

Example: A person attributing their prosperity to luck may not realise that others from less privileged backgrounds face systemic challenges in accessing quality education, healthcare, and job opportunities.

This ignores systemic inequalities and denies the roles of factors such as social class, race, gender, and access to resources in determining one's life outcome.

This is a privilege problem.

Manifestation techniques all do tend to minimise the struggles and challenges faced by others.

People do not have the ability to simply 'Luck' their way into a new life; some cannot get a lucky escape from an abusive relationship; some can't get lucky beating their terminal cancer diagnosis; some cannot up sticks and leave their hometown; some cannot escape wars; some are exposed daily to racial abuse; some don't have a smartphone to access help, or even know how to read this book. Luck cannot end poverty. It cannot end wars. It's true that everyone has a fixed amount of time each day, but we do NOT all have the same 24 hours, and all of our days differ in regard to the complexities of individual circumstances and responsibilities.

In the context of LGS, when we attribute prosperity to luck, we often fail to recognise the pervasive impact of structural barriers and discriminatory practices. This perspective places the primary responsibility for the success of individual qualities, ignoring the broader context of institutionalised prejudices and systemic inequalities that contribute to disparities in education, healthcare, and economic resources.

Strike the Balance: Manifest Change

While LGS has been criticised for overlooking systemic inequalities, Lucky Girls possess the potential to address and challenge these very disparities. By adopting an empowering mindset, setting concrete goals, advocating for change, and taking responsibility to create a more equitable world, everyone can harness the power of manifestation to work towards a fairer society. The key lies in integrating manifestation practices with awareness of one's privilege, systemic issue, fostering collective action with an intersectional perspective.

Uncovering the hidden layers that contribute to the privilege perception Lucky Girl Syndrome creates, and shedding light on the societal constructs that perpetuate disparities and reinforce stereotypes form a critical aspect of this exploration. By delving into the nuanced dynamics of privilege, the aim is to create a deeper understanding of the factors that shape perceptions and experiences of luck.

If you are privileged, it essentially means these 'luck events' come easier to you, and it's certainly far less challenging to 'attract' your manifestations than the majority who do not have the luxury of privilege.

Addressing systemic inequalities requires acknowledging the interconnectedness of various forms of discrimination and oppression. Any tool in the form of manifesting can be enriched by adopting an intersectional approach, which recognises how multiple identities intersect to shape individuals' experiences.

Recognising intersectionality helps to address the disparities faced by these marginalised communities and promote diversity and inclusion. Policy changes that address systemic inequalities and provide targeted support to others can help dismantle the privileges perpetuated by the LGS. By acknowledging and elevating the voices and experiences of others, we can build a collective understanding, challenge the conventional narrative of effortless luck, and create a more inclusive, supportive, and empowering environment for all.

In the pursuit of change, we must adopt all sense of solidarity.

Lucky Girl Syndrome is so much more than personal gain. Later, we will discuss how to spread your Lucky Girl powers, but for now, set an intention to share any techniques or practices you learn with those around you, especially those who may not have access to this information.

Don't Downplay Your Efforts

There's a common tendency to underestimate the role of personal effort when luck enters the equation. Some individuals lean heavily towards the belief that luck singularly dictates positive outcomes, sidelining their agency in terms of seizing opportunities and leveraging their unique strengths. Luck may present openings, but making the most of those opportunities necessitates active participation and strategic planning on your end.

That's why it's important to recognise that personal effort and strategy are intertwined with luck. Luck may provide opportunities, but seizing those opportunities requires your input.

Downplaying the contributions of your hard work and determination in bringing you to your current position undermines the value of your journey. Neglecting the dedication that takes place behind the scenes inhibits personal growth and casts a shadow over your potential for future accomplishments and generates a stagnant mindset.

Strike the Balance: Celebrate

Your goals and desires at times may seem so out of reach, but never undermine the effort and dedication that you have already put in.

Even before picking up this book and reading through the first few pages, you have already come so far so:

*Celebrate right **now** how f*cking far you have come!*

It's all too easy to get caught up in the pursuit of larger goals and overlook the steps taken along the way. By celebrating even the tiniest achievements, we validate the time and energy we've invested. This acknowledgment contributes to a sense of accomplishment and reinforces our commitment, motivating us to continue pushing forward.

Reflecting on our achievements and looking back at how far we've come serves as a valuable source of motivation. When faced with challenges or setbacks, remembering the progress we've made can rekindle our determination and capabilities. This perspective shift helps in maintaining a growth-oriented mindset and prevents us from feeling disheartened in the face of adversity.

Celebrating isn't about vanity or bragging. It's an act of self-appreciation and self-care. We deserve to acknowledge the effort we've put in and take pride in the strides we've taken. This practice nurtures a positive relationship with ourselves and nurtures a healthy sense of self-worth.

The fusion of luck and personal effort forms a potent recipe for success.

In the words of HRH Kris Kardashian – you are doing amazing, sweetie!

Is Social Media Is Ruining the Manifestation Game?

The art of manifestation existed before social media and influencers, with individuals using affirmations and positive thinking for personal transformation. However, the digital age has shifted the landscape of manifestation, facilitating open dialogues about mental health, personal growth, and holistic living. Social media platforms have pushed the concept of manifestation to prominence, motivating individuals to attract positive results. However, the emergence of Lucky Girl Syndrome on these platforms has prompted reflections on the potential for misinterpretation and illusory beliefs in manifestation. The double-edged sword of social media is evident in the realm of wellness and mental health and significantly impacts the manifestation game for several reasons:

1. **Validation Pressure:** The prevalence of picture-perfect posts and curated lifestyles on social media introduces a distortion to the manifestation process. The pursuit of external validation and the illusion of perfection overshadow the genuine, introspective nature of manifesting.

2. **Delulu Encouragement:** Platforms, influencers, and content creators that teach manifestation often miss the mark by promoting delusional thinking. Encouraging entitlement and irresponsible messages can lead to harmful consequences, taking the concept of Lucky Girl Syndrome too far.

3. **Oversimplification:** The spotlight on manifestation on social media has led to oversimplified techniques that ignore the complexity of human psychology and the multifaceted nature of successful manifesting. Setting intentions and visualising goals are crucial, but there's more depth to manifestation than portrayed in a social media post.

4. **Materialism Focus:** The promotion of LGS by influencers often centres on materialistic desires, neglecting the importance of creating meaning, purpose, and fulfilment in life. The emphasis on manifesting external gains like money or

fame oversimplifies the true essence of the manifestation process.

5. **Toxic Positivity:** Social media perpetuates toxic positivity by inundating users with overwhelmingly positive messages, often at the expense of acknowledging real struggles and negative emotions. This approach suppresses genuine feelings, making it challenging to deal with disappointments and hindering authentic chances of cultivating luck.

Toxic positivity, evident in the oversimplified promotion of Lucky Girl Syndrome and manifestation through positive thinking, is amplified on social media, often neglecting the truth and struggles of individuals. This damaging approach suppresses emotions, exacerbates negative feelings, and impacts genuine chances of cultivating luck. 'Toxic positivity' arises when negative emotions are disregarded, hindering the ability to cope with disappointment. The inadvertent alignment of LGS and manifestation with toxic positivity perpetuates a culture of fake happiness and contributes to an unhealthy mentality around mental well-being. While social media inspires, the downside is the potential for super-positive messages to worsen personal struggles. Genuine acknowledgment and open discussions about struggles are crucial for true growth and healing. Consider the impact of toxic positivity not just on recipients but also on those posting such messages.

Strike a Balance: Change Your Relationship with Social

OK, time to stop bashing social.

In the contemporary world, digital connectivity reigns supreme, with social media seamlessly integrated into our lives. These platforms offer unparalleled opportunities for connecting, expressing creativity, sharing information, and communicating, all while delivering an enjoyable experience. Just think about it – the fact that you can initiate a business with a single click on your smartphone, rendering the need for a traditional office space, staff, tools, etc. is virtually insane!

I may have sounded like the biggest hypocrite highlighting the bullshit of social media because a large majority of my life is spent on these platforms, and an even larger portion is spent helping others' well-being, and a lot of that is through social!

Certainly, I genuinely embrace my digital presence. However, my relationship with it has undergone a significant transformation – a necessary shift, as it had become rather unhealthy. Social media had the ability to trigger me, and perhaps you can relate to this as well. Remember, these platforms predominantly showcase life's highlights, often evoking feelings of FOMO and inadequacy. An abundance of studies has delved into the correlation between social media and jealousy. One study, in particular, focused on romantic relationships, revealing that frequent social media users tend to be more susceptible to jealousy due to various factors. These factors encompass the visibility of their partner's interactions with others, exposure to attractive profiles, and the inclination to compare their own relationships with those portrayed on social media.[9]

Social media has had a profound impact, and I am grateful for it. Because of social media, I found a career, and it paved the way for my career trajectory. Because of social media, I've been able to help grow my business. Because of social media, I've made genuine connections that've turned into authentic relationships. I'm able to keep up to date with trends, news, and family, and be entertained and educated.

Having immersed myself in this arena for over seven years through work and pleasure, I've encountered both the shadows and the highlights, the valleys and the peaks. But in all this, it's important to underline how you can use social media for good and at the same time protect your mental health.

Reclaim control over your relationship with social media, reshape your interactions, and guide your online experiences more effectively by . . .

- **Mindful Consumption:** Balancing online and offline realities. When we approach our social media usage mindfully, we're more likely to make conscious choices about what we consume and how much time we spend online. By setting specific time boundaries for social media usage, we can reduce the risk of falling into the comparison trap and prioritise activities that enrich our lives beyond the screen. Use a time management app for monitoring your screen time and setting usage limits for social media. These apps promote self-awareness and empower you to allocate your time more intentionally, striking a balance between online interactions and other aspects of life.

Be mindful of what you do see on social, may not necessarily be an extract portrayal of real life. Understand that people often present curated and idealised versions of their lives on social media. Avoid comparing your relationship to what you see online, as it may not reflect reality accurately.

- **Cut the Content Crap:** Being the basic bitch I am, I love a good quote, especially on social media. When the line is blurry between inspiration and toxic positivity is where you can get into a bit of a mess.

Want to cut the toxic positivity content BS out of your life? It's actually pretty hard – hard to spot, hard to ignore.

First, know that it's OK not to be OK and it's more than OK for you to express that. This is how we end the stigma. This is how we change the narrative. This is how you save a life.

Be careful what you are exposing yourself to, and don't engage in overly forced positive posts.

We should strive to always have real and honest conversations about the struggles we are experiencing. We should always be open to listening to those around us, not suppressing and silencing real feelings by forcing positivity on others.

Spot the potentially detrimental effects of toxic positivity on your mental well-being. Strive to shield yourself from content that could prove harmful to your psychological health.

This fervent emphasis on maintaining a positive outlook, coupled with the pressure to manifest an ostensibly flawless life, can inherit feelings of inadequacy, guilt, and shame. It can also add a perception of individual responsibility for circumstances often beyond one's control, thereby magnifying anxieties you may already be grappling with.

Toxic posts can be mitigated by adopting a more balanced perspective on your emotions. Allowing yourself to experience the full range of emotions – including what you perceive as 'negative' ones –can enhance your mental and emotional well-being. That is the healthiest coping strategy here.

· **Curate Your Feed:** Shape your digital environment. Your social media feed is a reflection of your interests, values, and aspirations. For a healthier connection with social media, curate your feed by unfollowing accounts that induce negative emotions or promote unrealistic standards. Social is all algorithm based. Make your feed more diverse so you are exposed to more genuine, realistic, and natural content. Focus on following accounts that share educational, inspirational, or thought-provoking content. Interact with creators who provide a balance of positivity and vulnerability, rather than those who showcase constant perfection. As you refine your feed, you transform your digital space into a source of positivity, growth, and motivation.

- **Engage Intentionally:** Navigate the algorithm's influence. Social media algorithms are designed to tailor your feed based on your engagement patterns. However, this can create an echo chamber that reinforces existing beliefs. To diversify your feed and expose yourself to different viewpoints, engage intentionally with content that challenges your perspective. By doing so, you can broaden your understanding and break free from the algorithmic filter bubble.

- **Tailor Your Experience:** To safeguard your mental well-being, utilise the option to block or mute specific keywords, phrases, or accounts. This feature shields you from distressing or triggering content, ensuring a safer and more enjoyable online experience.

Many social media platforms offer features like lists and groups that enable you to categorise connections and interests. These tools help you streamline your feed and prioritise interactions with close friends, family, or specific areas of interest. By leveraging lists and groups, you can create a more focused and engaging online experience.

· **Share:** Sharing is caring. Studies have also found that connecting with others and sharing our hopes for the future can lead to better goal attainment and personal success. So instead of sitting alone manifesting, get out there and post about your dreams, passions, and insights with your connections and followers in a healthy manner.

· **Notification Management:** Regain control of your attention and turn off non-essential notifications. Notifications can trigger a constant urge to check your device, disrupting your focus and productivity. We've evolved into a modern version of Pavlov's dogs, responding reflexively to the illumination of our phones with the immediate urge to check for notifications.

· **De-influence:** A relatively new concept, the 'de-influencing' movement on social media refers to a growing trend where people actively seek to reduce the influence of external factors, especially those propagated through social media platforms, on their thoughts, behaviours, and decisions.

This movement encourages you to reclaim autonomy over your online experiences, focusing on authentic self-expression, critical thinking, and intentional engagement with content that aligns with personal values and well-being.

This de-influencing approach can certainly help you to wise up to the BS influencers, creators, and brands that are feeding you.

Additionally, when under the 'influence', firstly fact-check information before accepting it as truth and question the motives behind sensational posts and adverts.

- **Digital Detox:** When social media becomes overwhelming, it's time to disconnect to reconnect.

Long periods of engagement with social media can lead to mental fatigue and a sense of overwhelm. Incorporate regular digital detox periods into your routine, during which you disconnect from social media to rejuvenate, reflect, and engage in offline activities that fulfil.

Changing your relationship with social media for the better requires a blend of self-awareness, strategic engagement, and being technological savvy.

Let's establish a pact, commencing from this point onward, wherein we perceive social media for what it truly is. We will transform our association with it, identify instances of toxicity, and generate genuine dialogues that contribute to enhanced well-being in both our online and offline lives.

Thoughts and Reflections

Weighing up the balance and the bullshit, and looking at both sides of the argument, hopefully you have become clearer on the peaks and pitfalls of the manifesting sphere.

There is no denying Lucky Girl Syndrome talks a lot of bullshit, and the BS highlights the need for a more balanced approach to promoting LGS, not only on social media but also in how we teach and portray the technique to the world.

Manifestation is a controversial concept divided by opinions—of which we are all entitled to.

Sceptics' reluctance to embrace the theory is understandable, as they rely on verified evidence before accepting new ideas. While some case studies support the idea of the Lucky Girl Syndrome and manifestation methods, scientific research suggests that positive thinking alone does not significantly impact success. Moreover, sceptics believe that the Law of Attraction oversimplifies complex situations. Therefore, if you are still in the sceptical camp, you may have difficulty working with LGS due to a lack of sufficient evidence and scientific backing.

With anything in life, it's important to question it and approach with a critical mind. Manifestation is no exception.

Right now, you may not be buying into Lucky Girl Syndrome, or you may be fully-fledged, converted, and convinced. Either is OK. Why, you may have been fully on board and then examined the BS behind and are now totally turned off. That's OK too.

If at the moment you are still dead set on attracting a Lamborghini or becoming a multi-millionaire by the end of the year, so be it.

The true essence of Lucky Girl Syndrome is to create sustainable and meaningful outcomes that are developed with our values and purposes while remaining in a state of balance and. So keep reading, as we're starting to get a whole lot deeper. This book works with evidence-based approaches to help you with your personal growth and well-being, so you can step into a life of luck. In the following chapters, you're going to learn exactly how.

The work begins now, Lucky Girl, let's move . . .

3

You Create Your Own Luck

In ancient times, people believed the goddess Fortuna would spin a wheel that would dish out your fate and determine an individual's outcome of luck; nowadays, it is us who are those gorgeous, glorious goddesses that create our own lucky powers.

Luck has fascinated humanity for centuries, with countless stories of people experiencing extraordinary success seemingly out of nowhere. While some still perceive luck as an enigmatic force, recent research in psychology and neuroscience has shed light on the underlying principles that influence luck. In this chapter, we will explore the intriguing world of luck to uncover its mysteries and learn how to harness its power.

Let's Talk Luck

Up until now, you may have felt quite conflicted about how you perceive the notion of luck.

Surely there are bound to be many times in your life when you've felt like your lucky stars have aligned?

You might feel lucky when you win a game of Monopoly, check your account to find out an unexpected tax rebate has been paid, or when your period comes after you had great unprotected sex, or on a deeper level when you finally meet your soulmate.

Whatever your view is of luck at the moment, you're now going to learn the significance of proactiveness, willingness to take risks, resilience, and courage, so you may be rewarded with success, favourable outcomes, opportunities, fortune, and luck.

Fortune favours the bold, they say.

'They' have been saying this for years – way back to 195 BCE, when Publius Terentius Afer coined the term. This ancient Roman poet and playwright, commonly known as Terence, was a prominent figure during the Roman Republic era. Terence was enslaved and brought to Rome as a young man, where he gained his freedom due to his intelligence and talent. The phrase has since become well-known and is frequently quoted to emphasise the importance of bravery, taking risks, and being proactive in pursuing one's goals.

From slave to famous playwright – quite a lucky chap, wouldn't you say?

But if fortune does favour the bold and if success is not determined primarily by what life throws at us, but by how we choose to respond to it, why not take this as a sign to open your mind to the powerful possibility that fate is much more in our hands that we may have ever thought, and start to see that we do indeed have this power inside us that can design our lives to live any way we wish.

The Science of Luck

At first glance, luck is bound to appear as a whimsical, uncontrollable force, but recent studies suggest otherwise. Psychologists and neuroscientists have delved into the phenomenon, attempting to understand the mechanics behind this elusive force.

Scientists have been studying luck and its effects on our lives for years, and I am pleased to inform the sceptic in you that there is some interesting stuff in these bad-boy studies . . .

Luck Is Energy

It is a scientific notion that we are all energy – a fact no one argues with. But for some reason, we consider luck as a mysterious force, shaping the outcomes of our lives seemingly at random. But in actual fact, luck is much more than just a happenstance event; rather, it is an energetic phenomenon.

Ancient philosophies, such as Taoism and Hinduism, have long posited the interconnectedness of all things in the universe. According to these beliefs, the world is a vast web of energy, where everything is interwoven and interdependent. Luck, in this context, emerges as a result of the harmonious alignment of energies in our lives.

Just like the Law of Attraction, Lucky Girl Syndrome uses the premise that like attracts like. Our thoughts, emotions, and intentions emit energy frequencies into the universe, influencing the energy around us. Thus, positive thoughts and intentions attract positive outcomes, creating a cycle of fortunate events we perceive as luck.

Same for Karma, too – a concept found in Hinduism and Buddhism that states our actions create energy imprints that return to us in various ways. Positive actions generate positive energy, leading to favourable outcomes, while negative actions, they believe, can result in undesirable circumstances. This cycle of cause and effect is interconnected with the concept of luck, as our energetic actions influence the luck we experience.

When we are in sync with our intuition, it guides us towards lucky opportunities, acting as a subtle communication between individual energy and the universal energy. Intuition, often associated with gut feelings and the sixth sense, might be a manifestation of our connection to the energetic flow of the universe. When we tune into our intuition and inner guidance, we become more attuned to the subtle energetic signals surrounding us. This heightened awareness allows us to recognise and seize lucky opportunities that coordinate with our deepest desires.

Swiss psychologist Carl Jung introduced the concept of synchronicity, where meaningful coincidences occur seemingly by chance. These synchronicities are believed to be the universe's way of affirming that we are on track with our life's purpose and the energetic currents of the universe.

In the realm of modern physics, the principles of quantum mechanics present intriguing possibilities for understanding luck as an energetic phenomenon.

- **Possibility 1: The Observer Effect –** In quantum mechanics, this suggests that the act of observation can influence the behaviour of particles. Extrapolating this idea to human consciousness, our focused attention and intentions might influence the unfolding of events in our lives, shaping what we perceive as luck.

- **Possibility 2: Entanglement –** Quantum entanglement describes how particles become interconnected, and their states are linked regardless of distance. Analogously, individuals might become energetically entangled with the events and energies around them, influencing the luck they encounter.

Luck, traditionally viewed as an unpredictable and capricious force, takes on a new dimension when seen through the lens of energy. The interconnectedness of the universe, the Law of Attraction, karma, intuition, synchronicity, and quantum mechanics all hint at the idea that luck is not entirely random but rather an energetic dance between our intentions, actions, and the vast cosmos.

See luck as a form of energy, be encouraged to become more conscious of your thoughts, feelings, and actions and realise its potential to shape your destiny. Combine positive energies with your intuition, and open yourself up to synchronicities, and you may harness the energetic nature of luck to create a more fortunate and meaningful existence. Move forward with a renewed understanding of luck, not merely as a fleeting chance encounter but as a vibrant and interconnected energy that flows through your life.

Viewing the principles that underlie luck, you effectively unlock the potential to enhance numerous facets of your life – encompassing your daily routines, relationships, passions, and emotional connections, as well as your pursuits and ambitions in your professional career.

The Chance Factor

Our brains are marvellous engines of perception, tirelessly seeking out patterns in the world to mitigate uncertainty. The subtle interplay between our brain's sophistication and our persistent belief in luck deceives us with its illusory patterns.

Have you ever thought that after flipping four heads in a row, the next coin toss must surely yield tails? The truth is, the odds of flipping heads or tails remain constant at 50/50, regardless of previous outcomes. This cognitive bias, known as the 'gambler's fallacy', reveals our brain's innate tendency to seek patterns and regularities in the world around us.

As a major function of the human brain, dealing with uncertainty in the real world becomes an imperative task. The brain strives to identify patterns and regularities to make sense of the chaos, seeking comfort in the familiarity of expected outcomes.

Neurons exhibit a preference for alternating patterns, as the brain employs a fascinating strategy called 'regression to the mean'. This process corrects for statistically unlikely patterns, ensuring that our perception aligns more closely with the expected average. It is as if our brain nudges us back towards the middle ground, away from extremes, seeking a sense of stability amidst uncertainty.

Sun's research sheds light on the brain's hidden sophistication, revealing its ability to recognise subtle yet crucial statistical structures in our environment. Our brains are more adept than we previously believed, capable of processing intricate patterns and subtly guiding our perceptions and decisions.

Despite the brain's analytical prowess, Sun acknowledges the belief in luck endures, both as a scientist and as a person. The concept of luck, intangible and beyond manipulation, continues to coexist with our understanding of statistical patterns. It remains a mystery, eluding scientific explanation, and captivating our fascination.

Lucky Streaks

Have you ever found yourself immersed in a continuous stream of fortuitous events? This phenomenon is commonly referred to as a 'lucky streak'. For instance, imagine acing a series of job interviews, receiving unexpected promotions, and forming meaningful connections with colleagues, all in a remarkably short span of time. This sequence of favourable occurrences mirrors the essence of a lucky streak.

When we feel like we are on a lucky streak in life, it's exhilarating.

It makes us feel accomplished, motivated, energised, lifts our spirits, invigorates our outlooks – makes us *feel alive*.

Experiencing a lucky streak can be an incredible high. Every triumph, stroke of luck, or serendipitous encounter reinforces our belief in the universe's benevolence. Confidence soars as we bask in the glow of success, and a profound sense of gratitude engulfs us. Each positive event compounds the excitement, leading to a cascading effect that makes us feel invincible. Think Lucky Girl Lindsay Lohan in the movie *Just My Luck*.

During a lucky streak, feelings of contentment and gratitude permeate our being. We appreciate the beauty of life and cherish the moments that align in our favour. Gratitude becomes our companion, helping us acknowledge the people, circumstances, and choices that contributed to our streak of good fortune . . . and attracts more luck!

Then in the midst of these good feelings, deep in the back of your mind, a niggling worry may start to crop up that this lucky streak may end, and something may be lurking around the corner.

Amidst the euphoria, when that subtle cloud of worry appears on the horizon, it may make us start to question our lucky streak's sustainability. Doubts arise, and we wonder if this abundance of positive experiences is merely temporary. The fear of an impending downturn can dampen our celebrations, tugging at the edges of our happiness.

It's human nature. We are wired to seek patterns and anticipate future outcomes. In the case of lucky streaks, minds might overanalyse, seeking signs of an imminent reversal of fortune. The worry of 'what if' can cast a shadow on the brightness of our lucky streak, robbing us of fully enjoying the present moment.

Now think of the intriguing contrast presented by sexy Chris Pine's character in the movie *Just My Luck*[1], who finds himself in a perpetual cycle of misfortune. The plot takes a turn when he shares a kiss with Lucky Lindsay, resulting in a transfer of luck from her to him. This shift in fortune dramatically alters Jake's circumstances, but he harbours concerns about when this newfound luck might come to an end. As the story unfolds, both characters come to realise that the key lies in maintaining balance – a realisation that underscores the delicate interplay between good and bad luck.

Lucky streaks are an emotional rollercoaster in the funfair of luck.

There's a whole chapter of this book dedicated this but for now, know it's OK to worry while navigating a lucky streak. Just as lucky streaks have their time in the spotlight, challenging moments are an inevitable part of life. Impermanence allows us to savour the good without undue attachment while staying resilient in the face of uncertainty. Ease your worries with mindfulness; stay present and immerse yourself in the moment, releasing the need to predict the unknowns of the future.

Your ability to cherish the present moment will carry you through every twist and turn that destiny may unveil and help you revel in and prolong the elation that lucky streaks bring.

Are We Born Lucky?

The concept of being born into luck has been a subject of debate for many years. Some people believe that luck is predetermined at birth, while others think that individuals create their own luck through actions and mindset.

The definition of luck does vary from person to person. What one person considers lucky might not be the same for another. For some, achieving a particular goal might be luck, but for someone else, their family, health, or happiness might be the factors that make them feel most lucky.

Remember – Luck is subjective.

The truth about whether or not we are born lucky?

You are born a gorgeous, tiny, incy-wincy baby. A helpless, beautiful little thing. When born we can't pick who our parents are or where our home will be. Our little minds are blank slates and we have no opinions, beliefs, judgements, or dreams of the future. We are underdeveloped and eager to absorb the world's wisdom, knowledge, and experiences. It's a beautiful journey of discovery that awaits us, where we'll gradually shape our own unique perspectives, cultivate beliefs, make judgements, and nurture dreams of the future. As we grow and learn, our minds will flourish like fertile soil, blossoming into the individuals we're destined to become.

It is the miracle of life when we are born – and that's certainly a lucky thing. Even the statistical chance of being born is incredibly rare and intricate. The alignment of factors, from your parents' meeting to genetic combinations, Earth's conditions, and evolutionary history, makes your existence a remarkable anomaly. With this realisation, it shows the nature of how unique and precious every individual's life is.

So if we think of it that way . . . we are not born lucky; we are just born.

The baby born at the Lindo Wing (aka the Rolls Royce of maternity hospitals) is of course, luckier than a baby born in a destroyed hospital in a war-torn country. The baby born in the Lindo Wing could be starved of oxygen and live their life with medical assistance – *unlucky*. The baby born in the war-torn country could go on to become an international model and philanthropist (soon you'll hear Waris Dirie's story on just this) – *lucky*.

Lucky.

We could go on forever if we entered into the debate of whether or not we are born lucky, because **LUCK IS SUBJECTIVE.** Everyone has a different view and opinion on this.

The idea of being born lucky suggests that some individuals are inherently blessed with good fortune and are likely to lead a successful life. However, the argument demonstrated throughout this book with case studies and scientific evidence to back up is that you create your own luck through your own efforts, determination, and hard work. Thus, we cannot rely solely on luck to achieve our success, but we can shape our fortunes by putting our efforts into turning possibilities into reality. No one can *truly* guarantee success just by being born into a certain family or race. Of course, it certainly helps a great deal, and there's no denying, an individual's surroundings and upbringing create better opportunities, but it's that individual's own determination and hard work that ultimately lead to success.

For example, a child born into a wealthy family may have had a better education and access to resources, but that does not guarantee their success. The child could take advantage of their circumstances and privileges, feeling the need to not set goals or improve their skills and coast through life without any real meaning or purpose. There is a phenomenon known as 'The Third Generation Curse', which states that 90% of wealth from families is squandered by the third generation; it is also found that 70% is lost by the second generation (AMG National). This statistic shows 'luck', in terms of wealth, doesn't last forever, and although people may be born into financial security and opportunity, there's a strong chance they won't exit this world with the same level of privilege. On the other hand, a child born into poverty may face difficulties and challenges, but they can strive towards success and create their luck with hard work and determination.

In an analogy for this, life is a game of poker where players are dealt a hand of cards, which might not always be favourable at first glance. However, skilled players understand that the outcome of the game is not solely determined by the initial hand but rather by their ability to make strategic decisions, read the situation, and influence the game's trajectory.

Similarly, in life, circumstances and opportunities may initially seem unfavourable, but that doesn't mean one should give up or be defined solely by those circumstances. Just as a skilled poker player can turn a seemingly weak hand into a winning one through careful decision-making, adaptability, and a smidge of luck, Lucky Girls can influence their own life outcomes by taking proactive steps, making informed choices, and embracing this mindset.

The message is clear: Just as you wouldn't write off a baby's potential due to their starting point, don't write yourself off based on your circumstances. Instead, focus on the power you have to shape your journey. Much like a poker player, some players may have better starting hands, but a determined player can influence the course of the game and still win. If the best starting hand always won, this wouldn't lead to much of a game. The skill is in what happens and how you react to the hand you get. Folding and giving up on the first hand without even playing guarantees no chance of winning – when all the cards have been played, you might look down and see that, actually, if you had just played the game, you would have won.

This approach aligns with the concept of creating your own luck by actively participating in the game of life. Nevertheless, it's easy to fall into the trap of fixating on privilege as an obstacle. Constantly scrutinising our initial circumstances can inadvertently feed negative thoughts that stifle our potential. It's vital to recognise that the circumstances of our birth are not indicative of our worth as individuals. We had no control over the circumstances that welcomed us into this world.

What remains within our grasp, however, is the ability to shape our own destiny. We cannot alter the past, but we have the power to mould our future. Instead of dwelling on whether we are born with luck or not, we can channel our energy towards charting a course that aligns with our aspirations. By embracing a mindset of agency and focusing on the steps in this book, you move forward, transcend any limitations, and turn challenges into opportunities.

So, my darlings, as sh*t as your luck may have been, no matter how challenging the hand you've been dealt, it remains our responsibility to forge a brighter path. The game of life is an infinite one, and though your start might not be the fastest, with good health, we have a long time on this earth to capitalise on opportunities. Understanding the intricate web of privilege systems reveals a broader perspective. It's time to rise and acknowledge the privileges we possess. Starting from the bottom, having nothing to lose, and reaching for the stars, in the long run can be more beneficial than someone born at the top, slowly losing everything. By becoming aware, we take that first step towards creating a more just and equitable world and can also positively impact our ability to attract luck and manifest our own desires. Comparison is the death of happiness.

Let this book sow seeds of transformation for yourself. Becoming self-aware, flickers of truth emerge, and within this chasm, they help us reshape our narrative and find our life's calling. You can design and sculpt a life where the judge's gavel is in your hands alone – a life where the yardstick of success and luck is yours to define. A life where you dare to choreograph your own dance with luck, believing that the steps you take and the choices you make, can fashion your fortune. It's an intimate orchestration, a symphony conducted by none other than the architect of your own destiny – *you*.

The Lucky Girls

After a brief Google search on notable women in history, I am filled with pride to see that there are thousands upon thousands of results, detailing trailblazing women who have broken barriers, shattered glass ceilings, and created their own luck.

Even as I scan through my life, I am blessed to be surrounded by supportive, strong, fearless warriors who are all women. My Lucky Girls. My role models.

Their significance lies in their ability to inspire, empower, and challenge me. I could write forever about the impact these Lucky Girls have had on my life and how grateful I am to each and every one of them. I hope you can bring to mind some of the Lucky Girls that evoke the same feelings, too. Send them love right now.

Celebrating women who have created their luck is not only about recognising individual achievements but also about inspiring future generations, challenging stereotypes, and promoting gender equality. By shining a light on their success stories, I want you to be inspired and motivated by these Lucky Girls. Highlight their achievements and be encouraged to believe in your own capabilities and pursue your ambitions, regardless of societal barriers.

Marie Curie – the first woman to win a Nobel Prize. Her pioneering research into radioactivity led to the discovery of two new elements, radium and polonium, and changed modern medicine. Wangari Maathai was a Kenyan environmental activist and the first African woman to receive the Nobel Peace Prize in 2004. Amelia Earhart was an aviation pioneer who became the first woman to fly solo across the Atlantic Ocean in 1932.

These Lucky Girls have been brilliant and brave enough to be the *first* at something and have changed the trajectory, so women never have to come second.

These women, SheHeroes, if you will, among many others, faced immense challenges and opposition but persisted in their pursuit of excellence and equality. By breaking barriers and achieving extraordinary success, they opened doors in various fields, creating opportunities for future generations of women to dream bigger and reach for the stars. Let's look at other contributions by people who strive for greatness in their chosen paths and have created their luck:

Malala Yousafzai

One such woman, whose story never fails to bring tears, is Malala Yousafzai, a Pakistani activist for female education. Malala's passion for education started when the Taliban took control of her hometown in Swat Valley, banning girls from attending school. Despite the danger, Malala continued to attend school, and at the age of eleven, blogged for the BBC about her experiences under the Taliban's rule. In 2012, Malala was shot in the head by a Taliban gunman for her activism, but survived the attack and went on to become a worldwide advocate for girls' education. Her courage and dedication to education have inspired millions of people around the world, and in 2014, she became the youngest person ever to win the Nobel Peace Prize.

Dolly Parton

Darling Dolly Parton is an iconic figure in the music industry, renowned for her glamorous style, her hair up to the heavens (*the higher the hair, the closer to God*), quick-witted humour, and exceptional talent as a country singer. However, her impact extends far beyond the realm of music.

Behind the glitz and glamour, Dolly Parton's compassion and philanthropic spirit make her the bedazzling star she is. Dedicating her life to uplifting those in need, her 'Imagination Library' programme, founded in 1995, distributes free books to children, promoting early childhood literacy and a love for reading. She also established the Dolly Parton Foundation, providing scholarships and support for students in her hometown of Sevier County, Tennessee. Dolly has been a trailblazer in supporting women and diversity, collaborating with artists from diverse backgrounds, and uniting people through the universal language of music.

Dolly's road to stardom was far from easy. Born into a humble family in the Smoky Mountains of Tennessee, she faced numerous challenges and hardships from a young age. Armed with remarkable singing talent and an indomitable spirit, Dolly refused to be held back by her circumstances and instead, used her music and performances as a vehicle to share her stories and connect with audiences across the globe.

Dolly Parton's success was not the result of mere luck or her big ol' hair; it was the culmination of relentless hard work, determination, and a whole lotta self-confidence. She understood the importance of seizing opportunities, taking risks, and stepping outside her comfort zone. Whether it was venturing into acting, establishing her theme park (Dollywood), or creating her own record label (Dolly Records), she exemplifies an unwavering entrepreneurial spirit. Her philanthropic endeavours, commitment to empowering women, and ability to craft her own destiny demonstrate the essence of her character. Dolly's legacy is not just one of music but also one of compassion, generosity, and resilience.

Waris Dirie

Another remarkable Lucky Girl, warrior Waris Dirie, is a Somali-born model, author, and activist, who has made indelible waves of change around the globe. Born into a nomadic Somali family, Waris experienced a traditional lifestyle where FGM (female genital mutilation) was common and ingrained. At the tender age of five, she herself underwent the traumatic practice. However, instead of succumbing to despair, Waris displayed extraordinary courage by escaping her harsh circumstances at the age of thirteen. Her journey through the vast desert, facing perils and dangers, reveals her immense resilience and determination to break free from the oppressive traditions that threatened her future.

Encountering numerous hardships and challenges, Waris Dirie's tremendous attitude and tenacity enabled her to find unexpected opportunities. In a chance encounter with a renowned photographer, Terence Donovan, she was discovered and offered a modelling contract. This fortunate event opened doors to the fashion world, propelling her towards international success and fame as a supermodel. Through her high level of determination, Waris transformed herself from a young girl fleeing adversity to a prominent figure in the world of fashion.

Waris Dirie did not limit herself to the glamorous world of modelling. Instead, she leveraged her fame to raise awareness about the brutal practice of FGM and other issues faced by women worldwide. In 1997, she courageously revealed her own experience with FGM, breaking the silence that surrounded this harmful tradition. This disclosure catalysed her to become an influential advocate for women's rights, lending her voice to the voiceless and shedding light on the urgent need for change.

Recognising the urgent need for real change, Waris founded the Desert Flower Foundation in 2002. The foundation's primary mission is to eradicate FGM and support affected women and girls. Through her foundation, she has launched campaigns, provided medical and psychological assistance to survivors, and engaged with governments and policymakers to enact laws against FGM. Her work has contributed significantly to raising awareness and combating this harmful practice globally.

Warrior Waris's advocacy extends beyond the fight against FGM. She actively promotes gender equality, access to education, and the eradication of forced marriages. This fierce passion for change is an inspiration to us all. Her commitment to social justice has led to improved legislation and international recognition of the need to protect women's rights.

Mel Robbins

Mel Robbins, bestselling author and renowned motivational speaker, is known for her '5 Second Rule' technique that tackles procrastination. Despite her own battles with anxiety, self-doubt, and financial struggles, she confronted her challenges head-on. Sharing her experiences openly, she proves vulnerability is strength, inspiring others to face their struggles and grow.

Mel serves as an energising role model who inspires people to accept change valiantly because of her proven capacity to persevere in the face of adversity. She has a powerful presence that cuts through, leaving a lasting impression by disclosing her frailties and making changes via experimentation and inquiry. Her books, presentations, and podcasts enthral with wisdom, candour, and comedy. She's one of my best friends, and she doesn't even know it! Though she is blissfully unaware of my existence, she holds a cherished place among my closest confidants – she's like your big sister or mother figure – adept at delivering the blunt truths and sh*t you need to hear whether you like it or not and invariably injecting laughter into every podcast. It's hard not to fall in love with this Lucky Girl!

Zhang Xin

Zhang Xin's extraordinary tale from factory worker to billionaire exemplifies how she forged her luck through unwavering determination and sheer perseverance.

Born in Beijing during the Cultural Revolution, Zhang Xin faced adversity but secured a spot at Peking University, which became a turning point in her life.

Zhang Xin's move to the UK for further studies broadened her perspective and ignited her entrepreneurial spirit. Navigating the male-dominated real estate industry, she co-founded SOHO China, and reshaped city skylines with innovative buildings.

Amid the SARS epidemic and the 2008 financial crisis, Zhang Xin saw opportunities to acquire prime properties at reduced prices. Throughout her career, Zhang Xin encountered numerous obstacles, with the global financial crisis of 2008 being a major challenge that tested her resilience. Despite the setbacks, Zhang Xin always looked for opportunities, calculated her goals, and looked for new avenues to meet her goals she can persevere and stayed focused that created her overall success and status.

Beyond her financial success, Zhang Xin has been a proponent of social responsibility Zhang Xin has advocated for social responsibility and women's empowerment. She has backed humanitarian organisations and educational programmes in an effort to uplift those from underprivileged backgrounds by giving them greater possibilities. She has established herself as a role model for prospective business owners, particularly women, and demonstrated via her activities that making one's own fortune also entails supporting others.

Zhang Xin's extraordinary rise from a modest start to a global business star is proof of the capacity to make your own fate. Her story illustrates the importance of optimism, persistence, and dedication to social duty, and serves as further evidence that this luck lies within ourselves.

Sojourner Truth

For remarkable individuals like Sojourner Truth, luck isn't just chance – it stems from strength, will, and unwavering pursuit of justice. Born a slave named Isabella Baumfree in 1797, she triumphed over adversity to become a leading abolitionist, women's rights champion, and enduring inspiration.

Her early life in New York was marred by slavery's hardships. Defying her circumstances, she escaped with her baby in 1826, launching her fight for freedom and the freedom of others.

As Sojourner Truth, she fervently advocated for ending slavery and ensuring equal rights. Amid rampant racism and sexism, she fearlessly travelled, delivering impactful speeches and challenging norms. Her eloquent and impassioned words voiced a nation's yearning for justice.

Her iconic 1851 speech, 'Ain't I a Woman?' highlighted struggles of black women, echoing through time as a call for equality. Collaborating with activists like Frederick Douglass and Susan B. Anthony, she drove tangible change beyond rhetoric.

Despite adversity, she stood resolute. Her resilience and commitment are reflected in her ability to shape her own luck. Personal tragedies, discrimination, and racism didn't deter her from forging a more just society.

Sojourner Truth's enduring legacy ignites courage. Her story underscores that with conviction, we can shape luck and craft a better future for all.

How incredibly inspiring was that to read?

All of these Lucky Girls have made significant contributions to the world, and these are just a few of the beautiful stories women hold.

From fashion, music, politics, and sports to science, maths, and technology – in any given sector, despite facing significant barriers, women are changing the world. Lucky Girls defy systemic biases and gender stereotypes, challenge outdated beliefs, and embrace equality in all spheres of life, encouraging progress and positive change.

You, too, have the power inside you to be like any of these incredible Lucky Girls.

Learn from these experiences, receive guidance, and let's help each other thrive.

You're already well on your way!

The Debrief: Your Lucky Girl

Who is your Lucky Girl role model?

What makes them Lucky?

Why do you admire them?

What key personality traits do they embody?

Luck Is a Personality Trait

What do the sexy scientific studies and Lucky Girl stories all have in common? They've found that luck is not just about chance, but also how we perceive and interpret events and take action.

Let's take the example of Sam and Sumira walking to the Tube on their morning commutes:

Sam is walking down the street and finds a £10 note.

Sam is someone who considers themselves to be unlucky. Sam believes finding this sum of money is a coincidence and that this tiny amount of good luck they've just experienced is short-lived. It will just about cover her commute and maybe afford her half a Pret sandwich later (*sigh, typical London prices*). Sam doesn't see this as lucky and thinks, *Why could it not have been at least £100?!* Sam's mind drifts towards her lack of funds and never-ending bills to sort, sighs, then carries on with the day.

In contrast, Sumira considers herself to be a very lucky girl. She struts down the street and sees this beautiful, crisp, sterling £10 note. *Wow, how amazing! Thank you!* she thinks to herself, yet also sparing a thought for the person who lost it. Sumira believes stumbling across this is a sign that good things are coming her way. She has a firm feeling that her good luck will continue as she picks it up, smiles, and continues on with her journey. Walking a little further, as she approaches the tube station, she sees a homeless man outside. She stops herself in her tracks, remembering that crisp note in her pocket, and hands it to the man. Walking away, she still has that smile, knowing fully well that her small act of kindness has really helped a stranger out, and assured that good karma will come back her way. Sumira is confident that with that small act, good fortune will come back to her, multiplied.

Can you see the difference in attitude and mindset?

If the researchers who study the science of luck are right, two people such as Sumira and Sam with identical experiences may frame the same facts completely differently. And the way they tell themselves the tale will dictate not only how they feel, but also how others feel about them, and even their future fortunes. People like Sumira who are optimistic and positive tend to experience more good luck than poor old Sam, who is negative and pessimistic.

The luckiest among us are magical realists who can see the upside of downturns and consider how much worse things might have been. People who can spin a yarn that emphasises what went right rather than focusing solely on what went awry, ultimately create good luck for themselves and increase their chances of getting lucky again and again. *Don't you feel lucky to know that?*

Richard Wiseman, a professor at the University of Hertfordshire, conducted extensive research on luck.

He found that luck is not purely coincidental; instead, certain personality traits can influence one's propensity for good fortune. Wiseman found traits such as optimism, open-mindedness, and a willingness to take calculated risks are those of lucky individuals. These were all apparent in the Lucky Girl stories – they all created luck for themselves, by working their arses off, pushing through the darkness, persisting and preserving through challenges, and making opportunities – all the while remaining optimistic. They are fearless warriors who embodied Lucky Girl traits, demonstrating remarkable resilience, determination, and creativity, inspiring others to achieve their own goals, too.

In Chapters 5 and 6, 'Lucky Girls Don't Do This' and 'Lucky Girls Do This', you will gain further understanding of the characteristics you too can embody in order to step into the world of luck.

The Luck Formula

After immersing yourself in the remarkable success stories of Lucky Girls, it's likely that a spark of inspiration has been ignited within you. With that surge of motivation, it's time to take action and set the wheels in motion to shape your own luck . . .

'Luck is the intersection of preparation and opportunity.'

The quote above, attributed to Roman philosopher Seneca, is a solid reminder to us all that we must create our luck and not attribute success to chance. This is a scientifically proven fact. A fundamental difference between lucky and unlucky people is all in the lucky ones' perspectives, which is formed through mindset, preparation, and willingness to seize opportunities with purposeful action.

Lucky people generate their good fortune via the following formula:

Preparation + Opportunity × Action

According to the sexy science, to create luck, we're going to need a combination of all the above. However, in true Lucky Girl style, we're going to take the principles from this formula one step further and add a few extra drops of *spice* just to mix things up:

Lucky Girl Goals + Preparation + Opportunity + Potential + Mindset × Action

Learnings + Celebration

= Luck

No, you didn't sign up for a complicated maths lesson here – the formula is much more constructive and simple than it sounds!

Using the formula, follow the steps to set yourself on the path of attracting positive opportunities and seizing them with purposeful action. The Guide below is one of the cardinal insights shared in this book. The art of breaking down colossal goals into manageable, bite-sized tasks through this practice, helps overcome the inertia that often accompanies monumental undertakings. By dissecting goals, we minimise overwhelm and pave the way for incremental progress. The courage to take action on these smaller steps strengthens their resolve and cultivates a sense of accomplishment. This consistent momentum will then drive us forward, transcending self-imposed limitations.

Step 1: Create Your Lucky Girl Goals

Deep inside us, we all have crazy ideas and dreams. Those pie-in-the-sky ideas are great and can change the world and we must all have the courage to at least try to pursue them.

People must have thought back in 1843 that Nancy Johnson was off her rocker for inventing an ice cream freezing machine, but imagine the world we would live in without her invention? Imagine on a hot day not being able to treat yourself to a Mr Whippy!

Nancy had an idea and rolled with it, replacing the old method of turning a bowlful of ice cream mixture by hand in a bucket of ice, by creating a machine for efficient and speedy results. She changed the game for ice cream, and her invention is still used all these years later.

A driving factor behind this book is to encourage others to live a life beyond their wildest dreams but also to be realistic about them in the process. You, too, can conjure up a magnificent invention like Nancy Johnson's *(and it will be easier once you've reached the end of this book)*, so have those big, beautiful dreams with realistic expectations.

Your goals are your goals. They can be anything you want – 'pie-in-the-sky' ideas or something that may seem pretty trivial – it's completely up to you.

Activating a lucky notion takes place when the intent of your goals is noble, selfless, compassionate, challenging, caring, considerate, and, of course . . . fun!

Take time to reflect on your life goals and the areas where you want to create more luck. Whether it's in your career, relationships, personal growth, or any other aspect, clearly identify your intentions and aspirations. As goals come to mind, write them down in your journal or below (the list can be endless!):

My Lucky Girl Goals are . . .

1.

2.

3.

4.

5.

Step 2: Preparation

Luck favours the prepared. While luck may seem to arise unexpectedly, the groundwork for success is often laid through meticulous preparation and continuous effort.

Studies have shown that those who practise and hone their skills tend to be more successful and experience more opportunities.

Oh, that person's just lucky – indeed they may seem, but what's usually the case is that the person simply was clear and prepared about what they were trying to accomplish, so when a 'luck event' came along, they were able to recognise the importance of it and harness it to further their existing purpose and their 'life design'.

Identify the key skills and knowledge required to achieve your goals. Engage in activities that enhance your expertise and understanding in the relevant fields. This could include taking courses, attending workshops, reading books, listening to podcasts that speak out to you, or seeking mentorship. The more prepared you are, the better equipped you'll be to seize opportunities when they arise.

Preparation is all about the skills you **need** to **succeed.**

Step 3: Opportunities

Opportunities are often hiding in plain sight. We've seen that Lucky individuals tend to be more attentive to potential opportunities that others might miss. By staying curious, adaptable, and observant, we increase our chances of stumbling upon lucky breaks. Opportunities arise from being in the right place at the right time or actively seeking them out. Having a broad and diverse range of experiences increases the likelihood of recognising and taking advantage of opportunities. Train yourself to be more observant and open – adopting this growth mindset and developing a willingness to learn and try new things will further help create opportunities and new possibilities.

Attend networking events, join relevant groups or online communities, and engage in activities that align with your goals. Stay curious and be willing to explore paths you might not have considered before. Sometimes, the luckiest goals come from unexpected sources – always be receptive to new ideas and opportunities that may not align exactly with your initial plans.

Step 4: Potential

"Life is like a box of chocolates, you never know what you're going to get" (Forrest Gump)[2] – and with that, we will no doubt, face obstacles along the way. Adding potential to the formula, we can examine the potential barriers that could hinder our progress towards and create a build-up of momentum. A study by Duckworth et al. found that anticipating setbacks and obstacles can significantly improve the chances of achieving a goal.[3] So before diving into an opportunity, take a moment to evaluate its potential. Consider how it aligns with your core values, the benefits it offers, and any potential risks involved. Promptly identifying potential obstacles can help us prepare and strategise how to overcome them to maintain motivation. Not every opportunity will be worth pursuing, but by making informed decisions, you increase your chances of creating luck that aligns with your aspirations. Perhaps when an opportunity lands on your lap, create a list weighing up the pros and cons so that you can fully evaluate it, and then go back through each step so far, checking if it can, overall, help you take that next step to reach your goal.

Question *why* here.

Step 5: Mindset

Studies have shown that those who believe in luck tend to have a more positive outlook on life, take more risks, and have a greater chance to be open and attract opportunities that are better aligned with them.

Researchers have also suggested that lucky people tend to have a resilient mindset, where they view failures as learning opportunities and remain positive despite the setbacks life often throws at them. Successful people often recount numerous failures that preceded their most fortunate achievements; if you, too, view failure as a learning experience and not as a dead-end, you can transform misfortune into stepping stones towards luck.

Maintain a resilient attitude when facing challenges. Embrace the idea that every setback is an opportunity to grow and adapt. Cultivate resilience and positive thinking to keep your energy and enthusiasm high, even in the face of adversity – that's the challenge here.

Step 6: Aligned Action

When you identify a promising opportunity, calculate the potential, and reframe your mindset, this is where you take that decisive, aligned action. Trust your instincts, draw on your preparation, and don't let fear hold you back. Embrace the mindset that every decision you make can lead to valuable experiences and learning opportunities, regardless of the outcome. Aligned action provides clarity about your goals and the steps needed to achieve them. By aligning your actions with your objectives, you can stay focused and avoid distractions.

Luck loves action – avoid overthinking or waiting for the 'perfect' moment. Start taking steps toward your goals, even if they are small, and you'll increase the chances of lucky breaks along the way. Ask yourself: How can you really seize the moment?

Step 7: Learn

Learning doesn't just stop when you leave school. Life is a constant stream of learning. We are all students of life. Treat every day as a school day – open to learning what you can about yourself, others, or the world around you.

Not every action will result in immediate success. Acknowledge that setbacks and failures are part of the process. When things don't go as planned, reflect on the experience, identify lessons learned, and use these insights to refine your approach moving forward.

Lucky Girl is a method that can help you reframe and reset.

Reflecting on past successes and setbacks and understanding what worked and what didn't, helps you apply the lessons when moving forward. It's worth remembering this when creating your Lucky Girl Goals too!

Step 8: Celebrate!

Number eight is to celebrate! In the previous chapter, we found out that in order not to adhere to the BS of Lucky Girl Syndrome and downplay our efforts, we strike a balance by celebrating them!

Acknowledge and celebrate your achievements along the way. Each small victory fuels your motivation and reinforces your belief in the power of your luck formula. Celebrate milestones and use them as stepping stones to the next level of success.

Milestones, again, are personal to you – big or small.

Own your success, Lucky Girl.

There's a fair bit to take in when it comes to activating the formula. Lucky for you, the table below is a compiled comprehensive Guide for your convenience, outlining the process of refining your vision and setting actionable steps.

By referring back to the steps, utilise the accompanying table to guide you through this exploration, enabling you to seamlessly manifest and breathe life into your Lucky Girl Goals. Let the guide be your compass, seamlessly transforming your aspirations into reality.

Resist the urge to hastily complete your Guide right away. Instead, read through the subsequent sections of this book, absorbing each chapter's insights. At the end, return to fill out the Guide and allow your thoughts to flow freely. Remember, this is a profoundly personal endeavour. Your route to luck is unique to you, free from external judgement or limitations.

Perhaps even devote a separate Guide to each of your goals. Break down the process into manageable components, ensuring simplicity reigns. Most importantly, infuse this experience with enjoyment and enthusiasm.

To make your Lucky Girl Goals a reality, it's about combining everything outlined in your Guide, along with determination and positive energy. By setting specific, passionate, and realistic objectives and taking consistent action as outlined in your Guide, you increase your likelihood of encountering lucky opportunities that can propel you towards success.

Putting your LG Goals pen to paper will enhance commitment and accountability.

See the Guide as a plan. A study by Gollwitzer and Sheeran found that when people explicitly plan how to achieve their goals, they're more likely to reach them.[4] The Lucky Girl Guide outlines the steps needed to overcome obstacles and achieve the goal and works with milestones and timelines to keep oneself accountable.

Create a lucky loop: keep going back to your Guide time and time again. Add on, take things out it's a work in progress – your piece of art! Stay committed.

The Debrief: Lucky Girl Goals Guide

In Appendix 1 you will find a blank template where you can fill out your own guide, or you can head to https://lucky-collective.com/ to download your free copy.

Step 1: Lucky Girl Goal	To write a book				
Step 2: Prepare	Start writing	Create book pitch	Research themes for the book	Share idea with friends for feedback	Read studies on topics
Step 3: Opportunities	Update my LinkedIn	Get in contact with publishers	Pitch to publishers	Take a writing course	Improve online brand
Step 4: Potential	Create a living from my passion of writing	Help people in the masses	Make a commercial success	Leave a legacy	Another source of income
Step 5: Mindset	Work to eliminate limiting thoughts	Become friendly with the fear	Meditate	Affirm to myself 'can do this'	Visualise success
Step 6: Aligned Action	Crack on with writing	Tell people to reaffirm goals and keep me accountable and feedback	Set deadlines	Budget and set time aside to balance writing with other work	Take a course to learn writing skills to gain confidence
Step 7: Learn	First publisher didn't like book idea, but it's OK, I'll find another one	Mistakes happen	Missed deadline	My limiting beliefs don't have to dictate	Everyone has to start somewhere
Step 8: Celebrate	Milestone 1: Finalise book pitch and outline format and themes	Milestone 2 Find a publisher	Milestone 3: Have my book published	Milestone 4: Sell 500 copies of my book	Milestone 5: 3 people tell me that my book has helped them

Make the Lucky Girl Guide visible every day. Print it off and place it somewhere you can see it numerous times throughout your day. Put it at the bedside table so you can reflect first thing in the morning and last thing at night. Post it on your mirror, your fridge, your car, your wallet – anywhere you can easily check in.

Even make it your phone or computer wallpaper (there's also a concise free wallpaper-friendly version too – you're welcome!). Whatever you do, let the visibility of your chart maintain a constant and powerful connection with your Lucky Girl Goals, connecting you with your purpose and driving your actions with unwavering focus.

Don't forget to share your Lucky Girl Goals and plans with friends, family, or like-minded souls who can provide encouragement and support, as positive influences can attract more luck and beneficial connections, and who knows . . . they may very well climb on board or assist in showing you proactive steps you may not have considered taking to reach them.

Thoughts and Reflections

Overall, luck is a complex phenomenon that involves many different factors, an interplay of perception, personality traits, preparedness, chance, mindset, and action. We cannot fully control external events, but we can shape our attitudes, mindsets, and actions to attract more positive outcomes. Embracing optimism, cultivating curiosity, and being open to serendipity can lead to a life that seems charmed. Embrace the power of luck, not as a mystical force, but as a blend of science and sensibility that moves you towards a fortunate and fulfilling existence.

By adjusting thoughts and influencing actions with Lucky Girl Goals, luck becomes more than a whimsical concept; it transforms into an amalgamation of science, psychology, and personal development. Venturing forward, see luck as a powerful force, a potential catalyst for greatness, and a vital aspect of the human experience.

The true beauty of creating your Guide and spending time breaking up your LG Goals, it acts as a stepping stone so you can confidently move forward in the right direction, opening yourself up to more opportunity, taking calculated risks, and having the daring attitude to dream big.

And – *if success is not determined primarily by what life throws at you, but more by how you choose to respond to it* . . . that opens everything up. That means your fate is much more in your hands than you may ever have thought. What a powerful possibility that is!

You create your own luck.

4

Limiting Your Luck

You're well on your way, Lucky Girl, but can you identify the obstacles that might be hindering your ability to attract luck?

Manifestation practices such as Lucky Girl Syndrome serve as a great tool but without recognising your limitations and internal biases, you carry on telling yourself the same old story, which turn into real-life horror stories – further adding to the complexities of achieving your goals.

If you're struggling to get lucky, you probably aren't fully aware of where you are going wrong.

Working through this chapter, note the areas where you can make improvements and changes. With a little effort and a little tweaking, you can start to manifest the things you truly want.

Unpacking the factors that might be impeding your capacity to draw in luck, we'll engage in a process of dissecting any potential barriers and raising a series of questions – confronting the significant queries that demand thoughtful answers.

Grab your journal and work through the subsequent questions. As you work through, take responsibility for your actions and decisions, shift focus on what you can control, and let go of the need to blame anything else for your lack of luck. Engage with the 'debrief' prompts provided, allowing ample time, dear Lucky Girl, to genuinely immerse yourself in each query. Take a deliberate pause with each question, ensuring that you thoroughly explore and unmask any areas that require attention and uncover any underlying sources.

Actively putting the work in now, you work on an optimistic outlook, switch on resilience, open the flow of positive energy, and believe in your ability to shape your destiny.

Have Your External Factors Become Internal?

In the realm of luck, numerous external factors lie beyond our control. Economic downturns, natural disasters, governmental decisions, and financial crashes are just a few examples that can potentially influence our luck negatively. When these external circumstances become internal realities, you meet at a juncture where your ability to attract luck can be profoundly impacted.

Stabilising external factors with an unchained, proactive mindset becomes key to cultivating the luck we seek.

Do you find yourself constantly complaining and blaming others/external factors for your current state of being?

For example: 'It's my ex's fault that I hate men and can't find a relationship', 'It's because of the government I have no money', 'If somebody loves me then I wouldn't be like this'.

When you blame others, you are giving your power away to them. You are literally programming your subconscious mind to believe that others control your life and that you do not have the power to bring about positive and lasting change.

As a result, this act renders you powerless.

Take back your power and reclaim your authority.

Affirm your position as the master orchestrator of your life (because, darling, you are) and your conviction that you possess the capacity to bring about positive and substantial changes.

Navigating the intricacies of this dilemma can indeed be perplexing. How on earth can we not attribute blame to those who seem to play a role in our circumstances, right? Yet, it's imperative to recognise that personal agency empowers us to transcend these challenges, guiding us towards a path of genuine self-determination and the capability to mould our fate.

We must stop blaming external factors – people, circumstances, etc. – for impacting our luck.

We must stop feeding the self-serving bias.

Self-serving bias is a cognitive bias that shapes our perceptions and behaviours by attributing successes to internal factors and failures to external factors. Those who blame external factors, such as the government or other people, for their bad luck unknowingly fall prey to self-serving bias, which hinders their ability to meet goals. A bias indeed, but it's something that acts as a way of protecting our self-esteem and maintaining a positive view of ourselves. It allows us to preserve a positive self-image by attributing success to our own abilities, efforts, or intelligence while shifting blame for failures or bad luck onto external circumstances or other people. This bias allows individuals to maintain a sense of control and agency over their lives, avoiding feelings of incompetence or inadequacy.

Blaming external factors for our lack of luck hampers goal achievement in several ways. First, it hinders learning from mistakes. If we believe that our failures were caused by something outside of our control, we are less likely to take the time to figure out what we could have done differently. Attributing failures to uncontrollable factors discourages self-analysis.

For example, imagine that you are trying to lose weight. You start a new diet and exercise programme, but you don't see any results. If no progress is blamed on 'genetics' or slow 'metabolism', you are less likely to make changes to your diet or exercise routine. Quitting may become probable.

If we believe that our failures are someone else's fault, we may become angry and resentful towards those people/situations, which impedes us from moving forward.

Your own energy and happiness are too important to be drained by external factors anyway, so stop blaming them.

If you want more luck, then it's time to end the blame game.

How do you break free from the cycle of blame and self-serving bias?

Be gentle with yourself here, as this one is going to sting a little . . . it's **forgiveness.**

Forgiveness is the act of letting go of anger and resentment towards someone who has wronged us. Forgiveness is a form of healing.

When we forgive, we are not saying that what they did was okay or condoning their actions. We are simply saying that we are no longer going to let their actions control our emotions.

Research indicates a link between forgiveness and karma. For instance, one study found that more forgiving people were more likely to experience positive life events, such as getting a promotion or finding a new job. Another study exploring emotional liberation showed that forgiveness releases a person from negative emotions, such as anger, resentment, and bitterness. This enables self-focus and progress.

With forgiveness, you open your heart by releasing emotions that do not serve you. In doing so, you are better able to evaluate situations objectively, seek solutions, and adapt to changing circumstances.

Despite facing years of imprisonment and oppression, Nelson Mandela forgave his oppressors, seeking reconciliation and unity for the nation. His forgiveness and ability to overcome bitterness and blame played a pivotal role in South Africa's transition from apartheid to democracy – 'Forgiveness liberates the soul' (Nelson Mandela).

The parents of pupils at Sandy Hook Elementary School, who faced unimaginable tragedy in the wake of the school shooting, demonstrated an exceptional capacity for forgiveness. Amid their immeasurable grief, they chose to extend forgiveness to the individual responsible for the heartbreaking loss of their children.

These have been just a few examples, but –

If they can forgive, so can you.

The act of forgiveness stands as evidence of the incredible resilience of the human spirit. When you forgive, you are not ignoring or downplaying the trauma or its consequences. Rather, it serves as a method to liberate yourself from the cycle of anger and pain that often comes with such intense pain. It's undoubtedly a challenging process.

Overcoming self-serving bias and the blame game is essential for goal achievement and personal growth. Relinquish blame and forgive yourself and others. Holding onto blame only creates negativity and prevents growth. Forgiveness allows for healing and the opportunity to move forward with a clear mind and heart.

The Debrief: Press Pause Playing the Blame Game

- What are some external factors that I believe are affecting my luck?

- How are these external factors affecting my thoughts, feelings, and actions?

- What can I do to change my perspective on these external factors?

- Can I be open to forgiving these external factors?

Is Your Healing Helping?

Everyone on this planet needs to heal.

Healing is healthy. Healing is the new high after all (amen, Vex King).

But can we be 'overdoing it'? Are we becoming a little obsessed with the self-help sphere?

Self-help and healing are empowering tools that propel individual growth and provide positive change. We all have a right and a responsibility to help ourselves and heal.

Like with any high, highs become addictive, and here, healing is no exception.

Particularly when one experiences an initial positive impact, like the best sex of your life, the feeling of solving a problem, or experiencing a breakthrough is beautiful, compelling, and feels so incredibly satisfying. We crave to go deeper; we want more.

We look at other areas in our lives that then also need healing, which is great unless we don't let the constant need for self-improvement lead to obsessive tendencies, where one begins to only focus on their flaws, which can lead to decreased self-esteem and self-worth.

Research conducted by the University of California, Berkeley, has shed light on the potential drawbacks of an excessive focus on self-healing.

This intensified self-focus can lead to a phenomenon known as 'selfism', where individuals become engrossed in their personal goals, challenges, and needs, resulting in social isolation and a diminished sense of empathy for others. This is particularly relevant in the context of the current surge in social media usage. While social media has been instrumental in reducing the stigma around mental health, it has also given rise to a peculiar phenomenon where individuals tend to showcase their self-healing as a badge of honour, inadvertently fostering a sense of 'FOMO' (fear of missing out), among others. Paradoxically, this can also erode our capacity for empathy.

The study's findings resonate with the idea that an excessive focus on self-help can lead to reduced life satisfaction, a diminished sense of meaning, and a lack of purpose.[1] It's important to pause and reflect: Have you fallen into the trap of overindulging in the pursuit of healing?

Self-healing is indeed a valuable endeavour. This isn't a call to abandon self-improvement, but rather a gentle note to exercise moderation. While your journey of self-healing is essential, it should not be a replacement for professional assistance. Self-help resources and guides cannot replace the specialised expertise of licenced psychologists or psychiatrists. Despite the merits of healing therapies and practises and their valuable contributions, they cannot fully substitute for clinical care, especially for those grappling with severe mental health issues.

The American Psychological Association has highlighted that individuals who exclusively rely on self-help resources for mental health concerns tend to experience less improvement compared to those who seek professional help. This underscores the importance of using self-help resources as a supplement to, rather than a replacement for, formal treatment. It's vital not to let the vastness of self-help information lead you to believe that you are better equipped than professionals to address mental health challenges.

I've walked the path of healing myself, many, many times. Throughout the years, I've invested significant time, effort, and a considerable amount of money in experimenting with medical treatments, alternative therapies, and various healing methods. I've explored an extensive range of options – you name it, I've likely given it a shot. I had in my head an idea of what healing looked like and a preconceived notion of what the healing process should entail, and this misconception often led me to exhaust myself. I would tirelessly strive to attain a state of enlightenment where I could be completely liberated from all forms of anxiety. In my mind, I perceived healing as a fixed destination rather than an ongoing process. This skewed perspective caused me to set unrealistic expectations for myself. I believed that once I reached this imagined state of perfect healing, all my troubles would dissipate, and I would be free from any emotional turmoil. However, this approach only resulted in frustration and disappointment, and I would frequently find myself back at square one. It took time and a shift in mindset to realise that healing isn't a final endpoint; it's a continuous process of growth, self-discovery, and self-compassion. Changing my idea of healing has been transformative. It has allowed me to release the pressure of achieving an unattainable goal and instead focus on the incremental steps I take towards betterment. This outlook has enabled me to appreciate the progress I make, no matter how small, and to be kinder to myself when setbacks occur. Understanding that healing is an ongoing voyage has granted me the freedom to explore various methods, adapt, and evolve as I uncover what truly resonates with my unique needs. It's enabled me to shift my perspective from a place of self-criticism to one of self-acceptance. A lesson that growth is continuous, and that each step forward is a victory in itself.

Healing is not a 'one-size-fits-all' strategy.

It all comes back down to a matter of perspective. Healing manifests as a unique voyage for each individual, and we mustn't confine our healing to predefined categories. The process involves trial and error to discover what genuinely resonates with you. Regrettably, not everyone has the privilege to explore a variety of healing avenues due to various limitations, and not everyone possesses the luxury of delving into an array of self-help. This is precisely why I am committed to sparing you the expenditure of time, energy, and financial resources by jam-packing so much in this book, and additionally, providing valuable free resources on the website (https://lucky-collective.com/).

Recognising that the exploration of these methods might not be universally appealing or effective – and that's perfectly acceptable. There will be things you may not like or that may not work for you, and that's OK too.

The crux of the matter is that you hold the power to heal within yourself.

You are your own healer.

This book, the resources provided, and the wisdom accumulated serve as tools to guide you, but the true healing process rests in your hands. Your unique experiences, determination, and willingness to embrace change will be the driving forces on this ride towards wellness and growth.

Balance is the lynchpin in this endeavour (along with every point made in this book!). As with many aspects of life, excess of any one thing can be counterproductive. As the saying goes, 'Too much of one thing can be wonderful, but too much of anything is just too much.' Self-help undoubtedly sparks inspiration and motivation, especially when you feel stagnant, but beware of becoming mired in a cycle of perpetual self-improvement that hinders genuine progress.

Finding what works is hard work. Maybe there needs to be a Tinder or Bumble for healing, where you can swipe through and see what takes your fancy, then make an informed decision before going on the first date with that chosen therapy (*hey, there's an idea for someone – you're welcome!*).

Anyway, whatever you choose to do for yourself, make sure your healing is helping.

The Debrief: Helpful Healing

- How do I define healing?

- What healing practices or modalities am I currently engaging in? How often do I participate in them?

- Are there any signs of burnout or fatigue related to my healing efforts?

- Do I feel a sense of balance and progress in my healing? Why or why not?

- What healing modalities seemingly work for me? How can I incorporate them into my daily routine without overdoing it?

- Have I discussed my healing with someone I trust, like a friend, family member, or therapist? If so, have they noticed any areas where I may be overdoing it? What insights or advice have they provided?

Are You Jealous?

Jealousy is an emotion that can arise in humans for a variety of reasons. One of the most common reasons for jealousy is when we see others manifest super easily.

Take a moment and scan through your life. Who pops into your head when you think of someone living the life you would quite like to have yourself? Or just open up Instagram – chances are you're greeted with a gorgeous snap of someone living the dream.

Now be honest – what do you feel?

Even if it's the slightest ounce of jealousy, that's OK, Lucky Girl!

It's an emotion we have all experienced at some point in our lives – heck, I've felt it today (do *not* Google Margot Robbie next to Ryan Gosling!) but is an emotion, and all emotions are the essence of our existence, they are natural and normal.

Feelings of jealousy are *natural*.

When someone seems to be effortlessly living the life you could only dream of or seeing them manifest their desires with no problemo, it can be difficult not to feel a small portion of envy.

Why do we get like this?

Well, firstly, jealousy arises from a sense of competition. Humans are naturally competitive, and we often compare ourselves to others. When we see someone else effortlessly manifest their desires, it can make us feel inadequate or inferior. We may feel like we are not doing enough or that we are not as capable as the person who is manifesting their desires. This feeling of inadequacy can lead to jealousy as we become envious of their success.

Secondly, jealousy can arise from a sense of injustice. Sometimes we feel that we deserve to manifest our desires more than others. We may have worked hard towards our goals, while someone else seems to have achieved the same thing effortlessly. This can make us feel resentful and jealous. We may feel like life is unfair and that we are being denied the success that we deserve.

Thirdly, jealousy can arise from a lack of understanding. When we see someone else manifest their desires easily, it can be difficult to understand how they did it. We may not be aware of all the hard work and effort that went into their success. This lack of understanding can make us feel like they have an unfair advantage over us, which can lead to jealousy.

And lastly, jealousy can arise from a fear of failure. When we see someone else manifesting their desires easily, it can highlight our own shortcomings and failures. We may become jealous because we are afraid that we will never be able to achieve the same level of success. This fear of failure can be paralysing and can prevent us from taking risks and pursuing our own goals and desires.

Don't beat yourself up when you do feel a flare of jealousy. It is a natural reaction and a valid emotion. Understanding the underlying causes, you can start to overcome jealous feelings and get back to focusing on what matters, Lucky Girl: You.

And what we don't want is for jealousy to take a toll on our mental state, so need be careful of the green-eyed monster.

The Debrief: Tame the Tiger, Don't Cage It

As jealousy is a normal functioning emotion, we don't want to suppress and cage the beast, but work with it to tame and calm:

- Imagine a garden filled with various types of flowers, each representing a different person in your life and their accomplishments.

- Visualise a majestic tiger roaming freely in this garden. This tiger symbolises your feelings of jealousy and comparison.

- In your journal, write a dialogue between yourself and the 'jealous tiger'.

- Ask the tiger about its intentions and the emotions it represents.

- Respond with compassion, acknowledging its presence but also asserting your desire for a more positive and peaceful mindset.

- Conclude by envisioning the tiger transforming into a gentle and supportive presence within your garden, coexisting harmoniously.

- Reflect on how this exercise helps you understand and manage feelings of jealousy.

Do You Think It's Bad Timing?

It's possible to have bad luck simply due to timing – missing out on opportunities or events that could have led to good fortune.

We aren't all fortune tellers, or time travellers, and don't have a third-eye raven to predict our futures, so it's impossible to be able to assess whether the timing is an issue or not.

What we do know is that when you firmly believe that the timing is unfavourable and luck is working against you, you inadvertently set yourself up for a self-fulfilling prophecy. This means that your negative expectations and mindset can unconsciously influence your actions and behaviours, ultimately leading to the outcome you fear the most.

Divine timing is a belief rooted in the idea that there is an inherent order and synchronicity to the events and circumstances that unfold in our lives. It encompasses the notion that certain things occur at the right moment, coinciding with a higher purpose or universal plan. The notion of divine timing draws upon spiritual and metaphysical perspectives, emphasising trust in the universe's unfolding.

The process of manifestation and luck is intricately interwoven with the principle of divine timing:

- **Alignment with Universal Flow:** Divine timing encourages your desires and intentions to naturally flow with the universe. It promotes the understanding that forcing outcomes or rushing towards goals may disrupt the harmonious unfolding of events. With divine timing, you open yourself to the right opportunities that effortlessly present themselves when the time is right.

· **Trust and Patience:** Divine timing works with the belief that the universe operates in perfect order and that things will manifest when the time is right. This level of trust and patience allows us to stay committed to our goals without succumbing to frustration or desperation.

· **Releasing Control:** Divine timing invites you to relinquish excessive control in your life. While setting intentions and taking action are needed, forcing outcomes and attempting to micromanage every aspect can hinder the natural flow of events. Surrendering to divine timing involves a balanced approach of taking inspired action while also allowing events to unfold.

· **Synchronicities:** Divine timing encourages synchronicities – meaningful coincidences that guide us towards our desires. These synchronicities act as signposts along our paths. Being receptive to subtle cues helps us recognise and seize the right opportunities, leading to serendipitous moments that feel like luck.

- **Lessons and Growth:** Divine timing acknowledges that certain experiences and challenges are necessary for growth and learning. In the pursuit of attracting luck and in the race of life itself, we know we are, at some point along the road, going to encounter our fair share of setbacks or detours that, in hindsight, prove essential for our development. Trusting in divine timing helps you work with such lessons and view them as integral components of life.

Let go of the notion of *Oh it's bad timing*, release excessive control, and stay open to synchronicities, recognising growth opportunities within challenges – you will become better aligned as events unfold, and you will be led to a more harmonious and serendipitous journey towards luck.

The Debrief: Devine Time

- How can you incorporate trust, patience, and surrender into your daily mindset?

- Are there any areas of your life where you would like to release control and allow the universe to guide you?

- Write about any intentions or changes you'd like to make to fully harness divine timing.

On the Lucky Girl website (https://lucky-collective.com/), there is a divine timing meditation to help you move forward in moments of uncertainty.

Are You Living in Your Comfort Zone?

We all have our own comfort zones. That cosy, safe space where we feel secure and content.

In a world where a lot is going on, it's our haven.

In the space of comfort, we're not taking risks and we're certainly not taking advantage of the opportunity, all important elements for creating luck. Stepping outside it, however, can be uncomfortable and, for many, a pretty daunting experience. So we tend to stay put, play it safe, and decide not to dive in and simply don't take the risk.

A study performed by the University of California found that those who step out of their comfort zone frequently experience higher levels of creativity and confidence.

This is because when we push ourselves to try new things or solve new problems, we activate different parts of our brains, leading to the creation of new neural pathways. These new pathways can then help us to think more creatively and approach tasks with more confidence.

Another study found that stepping outside of your comfort zone can also lead to increased resilience and coping skills. Facing new challenges and stressors helps us to develop coping mechanisms and learn how to better manage anxiety and stress.

To change your luck, you're going to have to get out there . . .

'There' being that big, wide world that's on your doorstep. Yes, this is uncomfortable; yes, it's scary; yes, it's cringeworthy; and yes, it may make you want to throw up – but it's where growth and expansion will happen, in ways you could only ever imagine!

Lady Gaga, born Stefani Joanne Angelina Germanotta, is an emblematic example of stepping beyond comfort zones, taking risks, and crafting luck through determination and innovation. Gaga burst into music's forefront with her unique style, defying norms of fashion and artistry. She challenged societal norms of fashion and art, with bold and eccentric outfits that quickly became her signature. Despite initial scepticism, her unyielding dedication to her vision established her as a trailblazer. In a saturated pop scene, Gaga redefined the genre by blending electronic, dance, and rock, distinguishing herself. She was candid about mental health and personal struggles, connected with fans, and championed LGBTQ+ rights. Her 2018 leap into acting with *A Star Is Born* was a gamble that garnered acclaim and an Oscar nomination. Gaga's artistry rests on reinvention and change, showcasing her versatility. Each pivot posed a risk, yet she stayed captivating. Gaga embodies a Lucky Girl who rejected her comfort zone, forged luck through creativity, and stood for important causes. Gaga's legacy inspires daring to be distinct, seizing opportunities with courage, and achieving greatness. Her influence spans far beyond music, illustrating the power of risks and innovation in shaping remarkable achievements.

Imagine if Lady Gaga decided to stay inside her comfort zone and carry on writing number-one hits for other artists? I, for one, cannot imagine a world without dancing to 'Bad Romance'.

If you too want to be Lucky, then you'll want to pop out of your comfort zone from time to time. This doesn't mean that you need to be reckless or irresponsible, but it does mean that we need to be open to new experiences, things, people, and places, or at the very least try . . .

Throughout my life, I've always worried about people judging me. From the days in school when I'd deliberately play small to avoid catching the attention of bullies, to those moments when I contorted myself into the 'perfect' girlfriend, sacrificing my values and boundaries just to keep an ex-boyfriend's temper at bay. Even in the workplace, I found myself stifling my ideas and opinions, fearing my old boss's penchant for belittling me. There have been countless times when I've moulded myself into versions of what I think people will like me for.

My comfort zone became a cocoon, falsely assuring me of safety while, in fact, holding me captive.

This journey of healing and growth, chronicled within these journal pages, has unveiled a poignant revelation. I've come to realise that my comfort zone, once a security blanket, has been limiting me in ways I never fully comprehended. And as I embark on the audacious endeavour of writing this book, I've ventured so far outside my comfort zone that the shoreline of familiarity has vanished from sight. It's a terrifying voyage, and I'll admit there have been moments when I've disregarded the very tools I've written about on these pages! There have been many nights where I've wrestled with my thoughts, surrendering to the gravitational pull of overthinking and spiralling into worst-case scenarios, and days have been fraught with the weight of panic and worry. But through it all, I've clung to a flicker of determination. I've made peace with the fact that criticism will undoubtedly cross my path, but I've chosen to be proud of myself for at least attempting this arduous odyssey.

As I tread this uncharted territory, I find solace in a single thought: if this book touches just one person's life, if it provides even a glimmer of guidance or solace, then I've succeeded in my mission. I've learned that success isn't solely measured by the magnitude of the impact; sometimes, it's the quiet ripples that matter most. And so, with trepidation and hope intertwined, I continue to move forward, relishing the unknown with each stroke of the pen and each word that takes shape upon these pages.

A bit of tough love, big sister advice – you're going to need to get over yourself a little, toughen up, and push through.

We need to face those icks deep inside. We need to get comfortable with the uncomfortable, move, and venture outside even further. Stepping out, we become open to new opportunities and experiences, that we may have otherwise missed. By exposing ourselves, we can visualise and imagine the kind of life we want to create for ourselves.

When we take that risk and jump outside, and better yet, succeed, we feel a sense of pride and accomplishment, and how empowering is that?

There must have been at least one time in your life when you've stepped outside, tried, and it's worked. Was it as scary as your imagined?

Let that confidence spill over into other areas of your life. Let it help you take on new challenges and manifest your desires more easily.

Whether it's starting your own business, travelling to a new country, taking up a new hobby, or leaving the house in the morning – the next time you're presented with an opportunity to try something, take the leap, and see where you go. Who knows? You may just discover a whole new part of yourself that you never knew existed!

Picture yourself as Julia Roberts in that iconic *Pretty Woman* scene. You know the one – strutting down Rodeo Drive in your newfound luxurious attire, feeling a bit out of place but absolutely owning it. Remember how she faced those snooty shop assistants with that classic line, 'Big mistake. Huge.'

Now, let's flip the script. Staying cocooned in your comfort zone? That's the real 'big mistake, HUGE' one, waiting to happen. Don't let fear and familiarity keep you from relishing life's grand possibilities. Sure, it might feel daunting to step into uncharted territory, just like Julia navigating the high-end stores. But remember, she didn't let the discomfort stop her.

Think about the sass and confidence she exuded when she went back to those snobby salespeople. That's the attitude you need to adopt when facing the challenges of breaking free from your comfort zone. So, let those words echo in your mind whenever you're tempted to retreat: Don't let staying in your comfort zone be your big mistake, a HUGE one.

Be your own bold and sassy self. Hold your head high and stride forward because the world beyond your comfort zone is where growth, adventure, and success await. Just like Julia, show 'em what you're made of!

The Debrief: Comfortable with the Uncomfortable

Let the following questions develop a plan for venturing outside of your comfort zone. Go back to your Lucky Girl Goals Guide and let your answers help take shape.

- What are some activities that I've always wanted to try but have been afraid to do?

- What are some things that I've been avoiding because they make me feel uncomfortable?

- What are some small steps I can take to start getting outside my comfort zone?

- What are some rewards I can give myself for taking these steps?

Are You Letting Your Limiting Beliefs Dictate?

Oh, that's just my bloody damn luck – chances are a phrase similar to this leaves our mouths at least once a week, even for the luckiest of girls!

Recently, during a lunch date with a close friend, our conversations veered from cartoon characters we weirdly used to fancy when we were kids into the territory of her well-worn limiting beliefs and a defeatist mindset. I've known her for years, and her self-doubts seem to permeate multiple facets of her life.

In most conversations and interactions, the cues were there, subtle yet noticeable. During this particular catch-up, the very second we met at the restaurant and were told by the hostess there would be a wait for a table, she sighed and muttered, 'Typical'. My tension ratcheted up a notch, but I was careful not to let it show. As we progressed through the meal, more of these 'limiting' phrases peppered our conversations. And finally, over dessert, she hit the nail on the head with a defeated proclamation: 'Oh, it's fine, it's just my bloody luck' – bingo.

I knew I had to speak up; the pattern was too evident to ignore. While I understood her feelings and her need for a sympathetic ear, our friendship compelled me to address what was unfolding before us. With a deep breath, I ventured into the delicate territory, choosing my words with care: 'Darling, I completely empathise with what you're going through. I'm here to support you through the challenges and injustices you're facing. But let's take a step back and reflect for a moment.'

As I listed her qualities – a daily breath of life, the ability to articulate her fiery, strong opinions with clarity, and vibrant health and banging body (her bum is like no other) – I intended to shift her focus away from negativity and towards the positive aspects she often overlooked.

My intention was followed up with: 'Why is it that when you encounter something seemingly negative, your immediate reaction veers towards "I'm just not lucky"?'

I braced myself for her response, half-expecting her to reject my perspective, perhaps snap back in defence, or slap me across the face. Instead, her reply caught me off guard: 'Omg, you're actually right.' Her admission opened the door to a candid conversation about the interconnected nature of her limiting beliefs and how they were shaping her experiences. We then chatted at length about her beliefs about herself and the world, dissecting their origins and impact. Through this introspection, she began to realise that her beliefs were influencing her perceptions and, consequently, her reality. The space she found herself in was, indeed, a breeding ground for negativity.

'When we argue for our limitations, then we get to keep them,' it was concluded.

Because of my own experience with limiting beliefs, I was able to reach that conclusion. Our dialogue prompted her to also rethink her outlook and confront the beliefs that had been holding her back. It's a testament to the power of honest communication and self-awareness – the seeds of change are sown in such moments. Our lunch date became a turning point, showing how a different perspective can help start to dismantle the walls of limiting beliefs.

It's remarkable really how a simple lunch date with friends can lead to profound insights and breakthroughs in our thinking patterns. Friendship is a form of therapy for sure.

Sometimes, all it takes is a fresh perspective from a caring friend to help us see our own self-imposed limitations. No one likes a home truth but helping others in a gentle and compassionate way to identify limiting behaviour and thought patterns, allows us all to take a significant step towards reshaping our mindset and creating change.

And you may not necessarily need someone else to point this out to you. Perhaps reading this you can spot areas where your limiting beliefs come creeping in.

The little niggling limiting beliefs are beliefs that we hold about ourselves and the world around us that are seemingly negative. But they do so much more damage to the narrative we tell ourselves – they limit our potential to grow, learn and succeed, and get lucky.

Limiting beliefs are a result of our experiences – so they could stem from our childhood and upbringing, our cultures, and societal norms and then manifest in our lives in various forms, such as self-doubt, fear, insecurity, and a lack of confidence.

It's your limiting beliefs that are stopping you from living your best life and ultimately, stopping you from being a Lucky Girl.

The impact is significant. If you're sitting there now believing you are not good enough to pursue your heart's desires, you're probably not even going to try. Consequently, you may miss out on huge opportunities that can be hugely fulfilling and rewarding. They can lead to negative self-talk and self-deprecation, which is damaging our self-esteem and overall mental well-being and manifestations.

The BS we tell ourselves:

'I'm not capable' / 'I'm not worthy'

'I will fail'

'They will judge me'

The list is endless. Limiting beliefs, influenced by external factors like comparison and societal expectations, often undermine our sense of capability and worthiness for success. These beliefs can manifest as self-fulfilling prophecies, hindering our pursuit of goals and reinforcing the idea of inadequacy. These limitations deter us from attracting luck, based on the notion that failure is unacceptable and are barriers impeding progress, potential, and self-expression.

Tell them a big F-off!

Believing in our limitations leads us to look for evidence of them everywhere. To break free, we must acknowledge and release these constraints. Recognising and addressing such beliefs by becoming more self-aware is a solid factor to becoming a Lucky Girl. The exercise below aids in identifying limiting beliefs and actively reframing your mindset to confront and overcome them.

Note that the second row of the table is completed as an example.

The Debrief: Looking at Limits

Observe negative thoughts throughout the day and record them in the situation/thought column. Look for a limiting belief that contributed to the thought and reflect on its root cause. Work on overcoming these beliefs by focusing on strengths and accomplishments, and changing self-talk to thoughts such as 'I'm capable of great things.'

This awareness can help address and reframe limiting thoughts. With consistent effort, unlocking the door to your thinking patterns allows you to challenge negative thoughts and replace them with more powerful ones.

(continued)

(continued)

Situation / Thought / Trigger	Limiting Belief Theme	Root	Challenge	Replace
Can't figure out the new spreadsheet at work	*I'm not smart enough*	*Teacher at school shouted at me when I 'failed' my exam*	*I've figured out things before without knowing how, so maybe I can ask someone to help me learn.*	*I am open and willing to learn because I am brave and bold. I can do this.*

Is Your Inner Resistance Making You Scared?

I know darling, I'm scared too.

Life can be an intimidating ride. Its unpredictability is a constant lesson that both positive and negative events can occur, sometimes beyond our control. Fear is a universal companion; each of us harbours fears – some rooted in logic, others not so much.

If there's something inside of you resisting, it's going to be a significant obstacle for you attracting luck in your life. These rules and limiting beliefs can all be an obstacle to anything that you want to accomplish, i.e. your career, relationship, or personal life.

Fear, in its essence, is both an obstacle of resistance and a shield of protection. It guides us away from danger and helps us make safer decisions. For example, having a fear of heights prevents us from venturing too close to the edge of a precipice. Similarly, a fear of danger (like death) steers us away from reckless choices, like crossing a bustling highway without caution.

On the other hand, there are intangible fears that can hinder the pursuit of better luck: the fear of failure, of loss, of making the wrong choice, or of making the wrong choice at the wrong moment. These fears aren't as straightforward as avoiding physical harm; they're the ones that stand between us and our aspirations, paralysing us from taking the necessary steps forward or even taking action in the first place.

We need fear to survive – *sort of.*

Our ancient ancestors faced numerous dangers in their environments, from predatory animals to natural disasters. Fear triggered the 'fight or flight' response, providing a heightened state of alertness that enabled them to swiftly respond to threats. This physiological reaction, triggered by the release of stress hormones like adrenaline, prepared them to confront danger or flee from it, ultimately increasing their chances of survival. Fast-forward to the modern day, and society introduces a range of complex and often abstract fears. The same fear response that once helped us evade predators can now be triggered by social situations, financial uncertainties, or even existential concerns.

Cognitively, fear serves as a motivator for learning and adaptation. It is closely linked to memory formation, ensuring that we remember threatening or dangerous situations to avoid them in the future. This cognitive function allowed our ancestors to accumulate knowledge about their environments and make informed decisions to navigate potential hazards.

In today's world, the cognitive interplay of fear is complex. On the one hand, irrational fears and phobias can be counterproductive, hindering our daily lives. On the other hand, a healthy level of fear can serve as a protective mechanism, guiding us away from risky behaviours and prompting us to take precautions.

When we experience a constant stream of negative situations, our subconscious develops a fear of positive change. This fear can be deeply ingrained and make it incredibly hard to recognise, thus making it even harder to attract what it is you want.

It's a form of self-sabotage that insidiously influences various aspects.

Consider this scenario: Within your current job, a remarkable opportunity for a substantial promotion arises, offering not only a substantial pay raise but also the privilege of a company car. However, for someone grappling with a fear of success, the focus may shift from the advantages of the promotion to concerns about potential obstacles and unfamiliar challenges.

The fear of positive outcomes can be a breeding ground for self-sabotaging behaviours. The nexus between these two phenomena is robust, implying a complex interplay that significantly impacts our thoughts, choices, and actions. This relationship suggests a profound psychological intricacy. When we harbour apprehensions about positive changes, it can lead us down a path where we unconsciously engage in behaviours that obstruct our own progress. This intriguing interconnection underscores the importance of exploring the underlying fears that might be impeding us from embracing the positive shifts we deserve.

It's important to identify our inner resistance – that niggling voice inside our heads that tells us "we can't" and transform it into positive energy. It is this narrative that may be preventing you from achieving your goals... or even getting started.

Do you say things like:

'I could never do that.'

'I'm not smart enough.'

'It's too late to get started.'

Do you know what a Lucky Girl would say?

'Well, I'm not entirely sure how to do xyz, but I'm just going to try it anyway.'

We Lucky Girls may not get it right the first time, but our willingness to learn along the way and work on each step that gets them closer to their goal will eventually lead them to success at the things other people think are impossible.

Ruby Wax, a fabulous comedian, writer, and mental health advocate, known for her quick wit and playful attitude is one who gave a big F U to fear and challenged her inner resistance.

Behind the scenes, Ruby struggled deeply with mental health issues, including anxiety and depression. At a point in her life, her mental health challenges reached a breaking point, and she found herself in a state of rock bottom. Instead of succumbing to her difficulties, Ruby Wax decided to confront her fears head-on, bravely seeking the help she needed and pursuing an education in mindfulness and cognitive therapy, which led her to earn a Master's degree in Mindfulness-Based Cognitive Therapy from the University of Oxford.

Using her personal experiences and her newfound knowledge, Ruby Wax transformed herself into a mental health champion, becoming an outspoken voice for destigmatising mental health issues and promoting open conversations about them. She authored books on the topic and even embarked on an incredible stage tour that blended humour with discussions about mental well-being.

From her personal rock bottom to becoming an all-star mental health advocate, she exemplifies how liberating it can be to work with resistance and not against it. Ruby used her challenges as a catalyst for growth and transformation, channelling her experiences into a positive force for change.

Let go of the resistance, the fear, and the limitations you tell yourself, and break the rules.

There is a necessity to release the weight that's holding you back, much like shedding a burdensome load. Imagine this dynamic as a magnet with two forces against one another. Picture your mind as the positive pole, and the resistance as the opposing force.

This transformation might not come easily, but you, Lucky Girl, can recalibrate this equation. Just like reversing the poles of magnets, you can replace resistance with positive energy, shifting from negativity to positivity.

Never underestimate the potency of the iterative process. Breakthroughs, from cutting-edge automobiles to smartphones and even space exploration, have emerged from incremental refinements. Often, people are scared of the **'F'** word – not *'f*ck it, let's begin'*, but **Failure** – so they never actually start. Start by remembering this: every leap forward involves a continuous learning process. Just as innovation thrives through repeated experiments and enhancements, your mission to luck demands persistent efforts. Prepare for and make peace with the possibility of setbacks and transform them into stepping stones on your path to attracting luck.

The Debrief: Friendly with Fear

Let's get better acquainted with our fake friends, and fears:

Step 1: Name

The name of my fear is:

_____

Step 2: Explore

What is my earliest memory of this fear?

_____

Was it triggered by an event in my life?

_____

In what ways: negative and positive – has having that fear affected my life?

_____

Step 3: Appreciate

How has this fear kept you safe?

_____

Do you think it's possible to change your relationship with this fear?

_____

What would happen if you did?

_____

How is fear trying to protect you?

_____

Could you feel safe enough to let this fear go?

_____

Step 4: Action

To finally 'face my fears' means I will . . .

_____

Are You in It for the Long Run?

Do you *really* want to start attracting? Do you *really* want the wheel of fortune to finally start spinning in your direction? Then you *really* need to understand that it may not happen overnight.

You *really* need to be in it for the long run.

Be 'in it to win it' and get clear on what winning looks like for you.

We live in a competitive environment that emphasises winning at any cost. Nastiness and success seem to be a marriage made in the deepest depths of hell. This is borne out by the popularity of caustic commentators, narcissistic heroes, and public put-downs, particularly on social media.

We've forgotten what winning looks like. We've entered into a competitive arena, but we don't really know what it is we are competing for.

Winning can be defined in various ways, depending on your goals and aspirations. Whether you are aiming for personal growth, professional success, or achieving specific milestones, it's not solely about the end result; it's also about the route you take and the growth you experience along the way. Each path to success is unique, so define what winning means to you and stay committed to your vision.

Attaining success and meeting goals is a multifaceted process that engages a captivating blend of psychological insights, neurological mechanisms, and behavioural dynamics. The realm of understanding success encompasses a diverse array of theories and studies, each offering valuable insights into how we can optimise our prospects of achieving our aspirations.

J.K. Rowling, who only went and wrote the spell-binding Harry Potter series, is a great example of someone who stuck it out in the long-run and won big time! Rowling's first HP book was actually rejected by numerous publishers. Just think of how it must have felt to face that setback? How easy must it have been to pack it all in? Uncle Vernon didn't care about Harry, so how could the rest of the world?

Rowling eventually found a publisher who saw the magic of the story and was willing to take a chance. Despite the rejection, Rowling remained focused on her goal, and, in time, became one of the most successful authors of all time, selling over 500 million copies.

And another apple that fell far from the tree of their goals, was the Apple co-founder himself, Mr Steve Jobs. Jobs faced many setbacks and failures throughout his career, but through maintaining his focus and determination, he recolonised the computer industry and became up there with the most successful entrepreneurs of all time.

The Bible even states, *Let us not become weary in doing good, for at the proper time we will reap a harvest if we do not give up* (Galatians 6:9). Even if you are not a Christian, this ancient verse emphasises the importance of preserving and not giving up, even when faced with challenges.

Science, case studies, and spiritual texts all combined offer valuable insights into the processes that contribute to success. Incorporating psychology and neuroscience to enhance your likelihood of achieving success and 'winning' in our chosen pursuits and becoming a Lucky Girl.

May this be a pivotal point in your life to commit to seeing your Lucky Girl Goals shine through.

The Debrief: Win Like Winner

When Lucky Girls win, everyone wins.

Go back to your Lucky Girl Goals Guide and sit with the 'celebrate' step. This is the step where you pinpoint how you know you've met your goal. Ask yourself what winning really looks like to you.

Thoughts and Reflections

Unlocking your luck is a process and it's essential to recognise that, like any manifestation practice, it's not a one-size-fits-all solution.

As you've discovered, hidden within the shadows are obstacles and limitations that may be blocking your path to manifesting the life you desire. These internal biases and old narratives can often turn your dreams into real-life horror stories, making your journey towards your goals more complex than it needs to be.

If you've found yourself struggling to attract luck and achieve your goals, don't worry; you're not alone, and you're now actively becoming aware of them. Through self-reflection and introspection following this chapter, you can now more easily identify the areas where improvements and changes are needed.

Remember, with just a little effort and some adjustments, you can start manifesting the things you truly want. This chapter has provided you with the tools to begin recognising and dismantling the obstacles that stand in your way. Stay committed to your journey, and soon you'll find luck becoming a more frequent and welcomed guest in your life.

5

Lucky Girls Don't Do This . . .

As the concept of luck interweaves chance occurrences and personal choices, it takes on a subjective nature. While it might seem that luck is beyond our sphere of control, influenced solely by destiny and randomness, there exists a range of behaviours that individuals, especially Lucky Girls, intentionally steer clear of, recognising their potential to shape their outcomes.

It's understandable if you hold the belief that luck remains elusive, residing in a realm where our influence is minimal. However, a closer examination reveals that certain actions and traits might unknowingly contribute to diminishing our chances of being fortunate. By delving into these elements, we open the door to a deeper understanding of our behaviours and how they impact our ability to attract luck.

The first step towards progress involves acknowledging these behaviours. As you explore the following points, you may stumble upon instances where you spot these patterns in your own life. During these 'a-ha' moments of realisation, it's valuable to pause and reflect, extending compassion to yourself as you take note. This self-awareness serves as the starting point for initiating positive change.

Through the course of any given day, we all engage in 'negative' thoughts and behaviours, often without conscious awareness. Some of these patterns might be familiar to you, while others might remain hidden in the recesses of your mind. Yet these seemingly minor actions can collectively obstruct your path to happiness and success. Noticing them lays the foundation for transformation, as you commit to shedding these traits that cast a shadow on your potential to attract luck.

The subsequent traits highlighted here epitomise the characteristics that Lucky Girls consciously distance themselves from. Why? Because these traits, when left unchecked, can inadvertently sabotage our progress, dampen our self-worth, strain connections, and even lead us into the depths of negativity. It's essential to recognise that these guidelines don't impose rigid laws governing the presence or absence of luck. Rather, they serve as guideposts, helping you navigate towards a more fortunate and enriching existence.

These are not super strict laws, whereby if you do not follow them then you're not going to get lucky. Absolutely not. See them just as guidelines.

This chapter is not about forcing you into a predetermined mould. We're not asking you to change who you are. You are uniquely you, and we never want that to go away. Instead, take the following as learnings and opportunities for growth, where you shed self-limiting behaviours and learn more about who you are at your core, and let that come through and shine outward. By identifying, addressing, and evolving beyond these traits, you pave the path for luck to seamlessly integrate into your life, shaping your experiences in profound and positive ways.

Drop everything you *think* you know about what it means to be or not to be a Lucky Girl and move forward with a fresh outlook. It's time to redefine and re-evaluate your approach to luck . . .

Lucky Girls Don't Lack

Maybe a little extreme here, as we all are lacking in some areas of our lives.

Today I'm lacking in energy. When a student lives in their overdraft, they lack money. When a date cancels at the last minute, you lack plans for the evening. When a baker runs out of bread, they're lacking in stock. You get the point.

It's when we post too much attention to our lacking and zone our focus on what we don't have, we are inadvertently creating a scarcity mindset.

Attention goes where energy flows.

It all comes down to a poverty vs prosperity mindset.

A poverty vs prosperity mindset refers to the contrasting attitudes and beliefs one holds towards situations and overall success in life. A poverty mindset or scarcity mindset is characterised by an obsessive focus on what is lacking in one's life – whether it be resources, opportunities, talents, or a lack of confidence in one's ability to achieve wealth and abundance – often leading to a sense of scarcity and limited opportunities. On the other hand, a prosperity mindset involves cultivating positive thoughts, embracing abundance, and actively seeking opportunities for growth and success. By adopting a prosperity mindset, Lucky Girl, you are more likely to attract your desires and create a fulfilling life, yet by staying with scarcity, cognitive tunnelling narrows your perspective, making it difficult to see potential avenues for luck and abundance.

The driving factors behind a poverty/scarcity mindset make total sense:

- **Fear of Loss and Risk-Aversion:** A scarcity mindset can be fuelled by fear of loss, failure, or losing what you have. This fear-driven approach obstructs attracting luck and positive outcomes.

  In their book *Scarcity*, Mullainathan and Shafer[1] explore how this mindset affects cognitive functioning. They reveal that when individuals fixate on scarcity, their cognitive capacity narrows, impacting decision-making, problem-solving, and failure to recognise opportunities.

- **The Role of Self-Fulfilling Prophecies:** In their groundbreaking study, Rosenthal and Jacobson[2] demonstrated the power of self-fulfilling prophecies in educational settings. Teachers were told that certain students were 'late bloomers' who would excel academically. Consequently, these students showed significant improvement, demonstrating how beliefs and expectations can influence outcomes.

When we fixate on what we lack – be it resources, opportunities, or skills – we inadvertently channel our energy into a negative spiral. This mindset often stems from comparing ourselves to others, feeling inadequate, or dwelling on past failures. As a result, our thoughts and actions become infused with a sense of scarcity, making it difficult for luck to find its way to us.

The act of focusing on lack perpetuates a cycle of limitation. Our beliefs shape our reality, and when we continually tell ourselves that we lack the necessary elements for success, we set ourselves up for a diminished experience. This is akin to planting seeds in barren soil and expecting a lush garden to flourish.

To transform this self-sabotaging pattern, we must shift our focus from lack to abundance. Instead of dwelling on what's missing, redirect your attention to the strengths, resources, and opportunities you already possess. This shift doesn't negate the challenges you may face, but it reframes them within a context of possibility and potential.

The universe *cannot* shower you with prosperity if you are sending out signals of lack. However, if you work with thoughts of abundance and gratitude, you will attract more good things into your reality.

There is abundance that exists within and around you; this sows the seeds for a fertile ground for growth.

Breaking free from the clutches of focusing on lack requires mindful awareness and intentional rewiring of our thought patterns. Replace self-defeating thoughts with affirmations of abundance and gratitude – use the table in the 'Are you letting your limiting beliefs dictate?' section in Chapter 4 and keep going back to it. Over time, this practice reshapes our subconscious beliefs, aligning them with the energy of luck and prosperity.

The choice between focusing on lack or abundance lies within your grasp. Consciously choosing the latter, luck flourishes in your life. Shift your perspective from scarcity to sufficiency, to create a magnetic pull for fortuitous opportunities, allowing the currents of luck to flow freely in our direction.

The Debrief: Shifting from Scarcity

Ten Things on Ten Fingers: Hold your hands out, palms up. Begin listing things you're grateful for on each finger, alternating between hands. Feel the gratitude sink in for each. After, close your eyes, bring your hands together in prayer, and say thank you. Carry this sense of abundance with you.

Lucky Girls Don't Rely on Quick, Fix-It-All Solutions

We are all guilty of wanting things yesterday.

We don't like pain, so we want it to end. Being patient is not in our DNA.

When it comes to our health, finances, life, relationships, or overall well-being – how nice would it be if we could just wave a magic wand and have everything miraculously resolved and fall into place?

Sadly, we can't point our fingers like Sabrina the Teenage Witch and get our sh*t together – and it's a good job too, as relying solely on quick fixes can have negative consequences . . .

OK, a quick fix does provide temporary relief and can solve an issue faster, but it doesn't teach you coping mechanisms. Say we have a headache, and we take a pill to alleviate the pain. While the pain may dissipate temporarily, the root cause of the headache is still there. It could be a lack of sleep, dehydration, or severe annoyance caused by your pain-in-the-arse partner. If you don't address the root cause, the headaches of life will come back again and again. Likewise, taking a last-minute holiday to Ibiza to escape the grind and stress of the job you hate. Naturally, it will provide a well-deserved respite, and breathing in that salty air and feeling the sand beneath your toes may make you feel alive (*never underestimate the magic of a mojito!*), but you're still going to have to get your Ryanair flight home, face reality, and be met with stressors you went to initially escape.

I want to take a moment to celebrate my incredible husband and share his story as a quick example. A few months into our relationship, I learned that he was grappling with alcoholism. At his lowest point, he turned to alcohol as a way to numb his pain and find a temporary escape from his struggles. It's fascinating to look back at how his experience highlights the pitfalls of relying on quick fixes.

Initially, he wasn't fully aware of the root causes behind his struggles, and he turned to alcohol as a way to drown out his problems. This avoidance of the underlying issues led him down a path of temporary relief but didn't address the real challenges he was facing. Even when he became aware of the root cause, the allure of a quick fix still seemed more appealing than making lasting and meaningful changes.

Reaching rock bottom, he made the choice to go cold turkey, cut out the booze, and finally seek professional help, so that he could work with his root cause instead of masking it.

Through it all, it taught us both that quick fixes, while providing immediate relief, can easily become a crutch that impairs true growth and healing. Just like finishing a bottle to escape pain might seem easier at the moment, the long-term costs and consequences far outweigh that temporary respite. These quick fixes can become habitual, leading us to normalise them as a routine instead of creating solid solutions.

Contrary to prevailing notions, opting for quick fixes doesn't always equate to cost-effectiveness. While the allure of a swift solution might seem financially appealing at first glance, the reality is far different. Quick fixes, more often than not, function as mere temporary patches, setting the stage for further investments of both time and money down the line.

Lemon water won't make your skin clearer by tomorrow. Doing a coffee cleanse won't make you skinnier, it will just make you sh*t loads (sadly, been there). Enrolling in that course to make £10k by next week, won't make you richer, you're just wasting your money and making them richer. These steps may help to some extent, but inherently they can do more harm than good. While they provide immediate relief or gratification, they don't teach you how to build solutions or acquire positive coping mechanisms.

Quick-fix approaches might initially deliver a modicum of relief, but they're akin to a hollow victory. They cannot impart real solutions or equip you with effective coping mechanisms that help you with luck in the long term.

Rather than seeking fleeting relief, invest your time and effort in uncovering genuine and dependable solutions that will stand the test of time. Dedicate time to addressing the core issues and developing positive habits, securing a safer and more stable future for yourself. The long way may be the harder way and might require patience, but the rewards are substantial and far-reaching – ultimately leading to a more fulfilling and meaningful life. Trust me on this one.

Lucky Girls Don't Fake It Until They Make It

'Fake it until you make it' is a common piece of advice that many swear by.

The idea is that if you act like you know what you're doing, or that you're confident, eventually, it will become a reality. However, this advice can be problematic and even dangerous.

But isn't that a fundamental aspect of LGS?

In some instances, and I mean some, 'fake it until you make it' can be a helpful strategy, such as:

- When you act confident, you feel confident, behaving as if you possess certain qualities or capabilities, you can influence your thoughts and emotions, leading to a positive change in your self-perception and efficacy.

- It helps overcome certain fears. Say you're afraid of public speaking, you can start by pretending to be confident when you speak in front of a group. Over time, this can minimise the fear as you become more comfortable speaking in public.

Allow me to cringe for a moment while I recall a few times when I've been guilty of 'faking it until you make it'. One recent experience that comes to mind was during my sister's birthday trip to Bordeaux. On a visit to a local vineyard, I found myself not particularly engaged as I wasn't consuming much alcohol. At one point, I realised that my attention had drifted away during a discussion about wine. To re-engage and avoid appearing uninformed to the charming French gentleman leading the conversation, I decided to jump back into the discussion. I didn't want to come across as ignorant, so I opted to act like I knew exactly what was being discussed. It was during this moment that I was asked, 'Have you heard of Pier Something?' (To this day, I still have no idea what the actual name is). Seizing the moment, I confidently responded, 'Indeed, I listened to him on a podcast just the other day.' However, my attempt to sound knowledgeable was met with an unexpected disclosure: 'He *actually* passed away in 1906.' Mortified.

In earlier chapters, we explored the concept of daydreaming, often referred to by some as delusion. Delusion, in this context, embraces the theme of 'faking it until they make it' when it comes to the art of manifestation.

Lucky Girls don't do that.

Faking it is essentially dishonest – which does not align with your soul or your core values. Pretending to have a skill, knowledge, or experience you do not possess, can lead to misrepresentation and dishonesty.

Over time, that dishonesty can catch up with you and you may run into serious consequences, such as losing the trust of others, your job, and money . . . or, in my case, it will make you *cringe* every time you go to think about it.

Not-so-Lucky-Girl Anna Delvey (born Anna Sorokin) is the queen of 'faking it'.

Adopting the persona of 'Anna Delvey' and portraying herself as a wealthy socialite in New York with a trust fund and connections to powerful individuals, she gained access to elite social circles in New York City and managed to convince people, including celebrities and influential figures, that she was a wealthy and successful entrepreneur. This fabricated identity scored her luxury hotel stays, dinners at boojie restaurants, and invitations to high-profile events, all while running up significant bills and avoiding payment.

Anna attempted to secure a massive loan from a bank to fund a private arts club she claimed to be developing. Her web of deceit extended to multiple fraudulent schemes, leading to her being charged with several counts of grand larceny and theft of services.

Eventually, her deception was exposed, and Anna Sorokin was arrested and charged with multiple felonies. In 2019, she was found guilty of multiple charges, including grand larceny and theft of services, and sentenced to prison.

Inventing Anna not only led to legal troubles but also damaged the trust and reputation of those she had interacted with during the reign of scheming.

Similarly, the case of Elizabeth Holmes, founder of Theranos, is another lesson to learn from.

Founded in 2003, Theranos set the ambitious goal of revolutionising blood testing by developing a device that could perform a wide range of tests using just a few drops of blood. She presented herself as a visionary and claimed to have developed groundbreaking technology that would disrupt the healthcare industry.

Holmes successfully convinced investors, business partners, and the media of the potential of Theranos. The company garnered widespread attention and raised billions of dollars in funding, reaching a valuation of around $9 billion at its peak.

However, as investigations and scrutiny intensified, it became evident that Theranos's technology was far from what Holmes had claimed. Shockingly, the device failed to deliver accurate results, and the company was unable to deliver on its promises. The technology was not adequately validated, and there were numerous issues with the product. It was then later revealed that Holmes and Theranos had misled investors, regulators, and the public about the capabilities and accuracy of their technology. The company's failure to deliver on its promises eventually led to its downfall. Holmes faced multiple lawsuits and was charged with criminal fraud by the U.S. Securities and Exchange Commission (SEC).

Let these cautionary tales serve as a stark reminder that dishonesty and deception may lead to short-term gains but result in significant long-term consequences, and be a warning against falling into the trap of faking success. Portraying a false image, the truth will eventually surface and can lead to severe repercussions. Transparency, authenticity, and ethical practices are fundamental to building a successful and sustainable enterprise, and essential for luck.

Faking it until you make it may very well work for you in some situations, but in others, it can be a recipe for disaster. If you're pretending to know what you're doing without actually having that skill set, it's more than likely you'll make mistakes, and that can lead to poor outcomes.

It's a tempting shortcut to get ahead in life but by pretending to have or be someone you're not, you're not learning or growing. Growth occurs when you acknowledge your limitations, work to better yourself, and seek to acquire new skills and knowledge.

The need to 'fake it' will eventually take a toll on your self-esteem. Living a life that is different from who you are can lead to anxiety, stress, and feelings of inadequacy. If you fake confidence, you may start to believe that you are not capable of being confident on your own, or you may never develop a real sense of who you truly are. If you are faking being lucky, you are ignoring those little, beautiful elements that have already brought you luck and blocking for more luck from coming in.

Faking something is not the same as building something real. Lucky Girls attract real luck, which comes from believing in themselves and their abilities.

Lucky Girls Don't Compare

In our hyper-connected world, it is all too easy to fall into the comparison trap, where we constantly measure our achievements, possessions, and happiness against our peers. While some level of comparison can be motivating, getting stuck in this cycle can have detrimental effects on one's ability to create luck and achieve our Lucky Girl Goals.

Theodore Roosevelt, way back when he was president of the USA, famously said, 'Comparison is the thief of joy' – and it is just that: *a thief!*

This spider's web of thoughts and emotions facilitates the need to constantly measure ourselves against others. We compare all sorts – from appearances to achievements, lifestyles, and possessions. It can seep into any aspect of our lives.

Since comparison is a fundamental human impulse, there's really no way to shut it down completely. But if we understand what it is, the mechanisms, and what to watch out for, we may be able to mitigate the negative effects and amplify the good, both online and off.

At its core, the comparison trap can be defined as the tendency of individuals to assess their worth and abilities by comparing themselves to others. This natural human inclination to evaluate ourselves relative to those around us has been extensively studied in social psychology. Navigating through life, we often look to our peers, colleagues, and even celebrities as benchmarks against which we measure our successes and failures. Understanding the underlying mechanisms that drive the comparison trap is vital to comprehending its far-reaching effects on our well-being and mental health.

In this digital age, the need to showcase curated lives and glossy portrayals means social comparisons have reached unprecedented levels. The prevalence of social comparisons in modern society is a testament to our innate desire to belong, to excel, and to be acknowledged. From the pursuit of picture-perfect lifestyles to the relentless quest for validation, we find ourselves immersed in a world where comparison has become second nature.

Platforms provide fertile ground for the comparison trap to take root and flourish, as they thrive on such metrics as likes, comments, and followers, which serve as external validation. Studies have shown that comparing one's own life to the perfect lives portrayed on social media can lead to a diminished sense of self-worth. Moreover, viewing highly curated images on social media platforms like Instagram led to decreased body satisfaction and esteem among participants.[3] Another study found that users who engaged in upward social comparisons on Facebook were more likely to experience feelings of envy.[4]

At times, social comparisons can serve as a motivational tool, propelling one to strive for self-improvement, but the negative effects of the comparison trap should not be underestimated.

- **Healthy Example:** When I admire the woman on the beach with her golden tan and washboard abs and think, 'Wow, how amazing does she look?!' and 'Yas Queen!'

- **Not Healthy:** When I look down at my own body and start to criticise myself and think, 'I'm so fat and lazy for not hitting the gym to prepare for this holiday' or 'Why can't I look effortlessly gorgeous like her?'

The incessant pursuit of being an idealised version of ourselves is causing an endless cycle of dissatisfaction and eroding self-worth, and it mainly stems from comparison.

Social Comparison Theory

Proposed by social psychologist Leon Festinger (1954), the theory provides valuable insights into the mechanisms behind the comparison trap. At its heart, the theory posits that people engage in social comparison to gain accurate self-assessments and reduce uncertainty about their abilities and achievements.

According to Social Comparison Theory, individuals have an inherent drive to evaluate themselves in comparison to others, especially in situations where objective standards for self-evaluation are lacking. In the absence of clear benchmarks, people turn to their social environment to assess their skills, attributes, and personal worth. Festinger argued that this tendency for social comparison serves as a way to gauge one's own abilities and make sense of the world around them.

We often compare ourselves to others who we perceive as similar or relevant in specific domains. For example, as a student, you may compare your academic performance with that of your classmates; or at work, you might compare your professional accomplishments with those of your colleagues. These comparisons can lead to both upward and downward social comparisons:

- **Upward Social Comparison:** Comparing to others perceived as superior or more successful. While upward comparisons can provide motivation and inspiration to improve, they may cause feelings of inadequacy where people feel they fall short in comparison.

- **Downward Social Comparison:** Comparing to others perceived as less successful or less fortunate. Engaging in downward comparisons can boost self-esteem and provide a sense of relief or comfort in one's current situation.

Lucky Girls don't compare up or down and do not measure their worth against idealised representations.

Break Free from the Trap

Going forward, instead of using others as a measuring stick, set your own Lucky Girl Goals and benchmarks based on your unique values and aspirations. Celebrate your own progress, regardless of how it compares to those around you; develop a sense of accomplishment for all you do; and work on feeling content with what you have and who you are. Embrace your individuality and appreciate your strengths and abilities, Lucky Girl. All this will help you liberate yourself from the comparison trap and pursue your luck and dreams without the burden of unrealistic expectations.

Lucky Girls Don't Drain

Lucky Girls do care what others think, in terms of being mindful of how they are perceived to avoid appearing ignorant or entitled, but they don't drain others nor let others drain them.

Energy is a contagious force.

Remaining vigilant against external negativity when engaging in the practice of manifesting is incredibly important for safeguarding your intentions and aspirations. Make no mistake, in the pursuit of manifesting dreams and goals, you're going to encounter scepticism, doubt, or even outright criticism from others – whether they say it to your face or behind your back is another thing!

Watch Out for Energy Vampires

Energy vampires LOVE to swallow up every injustice in the world and spit back their venom of blame. They are people who possess the uncanny ability to sap the vitality and positivity of those around them. *You know who they are!*

These emotional leeches can leave us feeling drained, exhausted, and disheartened.

The vampires often lurk in plain sight, camouflaging themselves beneath a veneer of friendliness or charm. They can manifest as incessant complainers, perpetual victims, or those who thrive on drama. They literally suck your blood and seek to replenish it by syphoning off the energy of others. This parasitic exchange can leave us feeling emotionally depleted, leading to anxiety, stress, and even physical exhaustion.

Recognising these traits can help us discern when we're encountering an energy vampire or if we're acting like one.

No, you're not going to have to start wearing a garlic necklace or carry a stake to put through the vampire's heart, but you can protect your emotional fatigue, productivity, and outlook on life by:

- **Protecting Your Energy:** Defending against energy vampires requires a multifaceted approach. Firstly, setting emotional boundaries is essential. Learning to say 'no' to excessive demands and avoiding being drawn into their negative narratives is crucial. Secondly, practising self-care through meditation, mindfulness, and activities that rejuvenate your own energy can help replenish any losses.

- **Request Boundaries:** One of the biggest revelations I had once was a therapist telling me you cannot set boundaries for other people – you request them.

  Setting boundaries implies that you directly dictate or control the actions of others – which you don't. You do, however, have the power to establish and communicate your own boundaries. Instead of imposing limits on someone else's behaviour, you can express your needs and expectations through open and respectful communication.

Politely but firmly establish boundaries with those who undermine your efforts, and regulate your emotional well-being.

When you request boundaries, you're asking others to respect your needs. Express your feelings and concerns clearly. Sharing boundaries lets others see your perspective and adjust their behaviours. You can't control their adherence, but encouraging open communication is the first step.

Healthy boundaries go both ways; others can express them too. Respect boundaries, listen to your emotions, build back up trust, form a mutual understanding, and you'll notice an improvement in your relationships.

- **Exclude External Influences:** The opinions of others can exert a significant influence on our thoughts and emotions. Negative comments or scepticism from others might make you second guess yourself and feel self-doubt, but know that these external voices do not define your potential. Flip the switch and shield yourself from their impact – maybe their negativity stems from their own limitations?

- **Protect Your Vision:** When others cast doubt on your aspirations, it can weaken your resolve and diminish your confidence in the process. Being aware of the potential for negativity allows you to fortify your manifesting beliefs and protect the vision you're striving to bring into reality.

- **Internal Resilience:** Building emotional resilience equips you with the tools to combat the draining effects of energy vampires. Put your learnings in this book into practice. You are learning how to develop a strong sense of self-worth, practise emotional detachment, and focus on personal growth, and all the strategies outlined in these pages will help you remain unfazed by others' negativity. Developing inner resilience is key to combating the effects of others tearing you down. Strengthen your self-belief, maintain positive self-talk, and reflect on past achievements and capabilities. This internal armour shields you from the doubts and criticisms of others, re-aligning you with your manifesting goals.

- **Positive People:** Surrounding yourself with positive individuals who uplift, support, and inspire you is a powerful defence against energy vampires. Cultivating a circle of friends, family, and colleagues who share your positive outlook and contribute to your emotional well-being acts as a buffer against the draining influence of energy vampires.

- **Selective Sharing:** Not everyone needs to be privy to your manifesting. Choose whom you share your aspirations with wisely. Share with those who genuinely support and encourage your growth, while protecting your dreams from those who may inadvertently bring negativity.

- **Focus on Results:** Redirect your attention away from negativity and towards the results you are manifesting. When you see your intentions materialising and your efforts bearing fruit, it becomes easier to dismiss external doubt and stay committed to your path.

Lucky Girls don't allow others to continue to tear them down. Maintain your energy and emotional equilibrium by minimising the presence of others' negative influences and shielding from their draining influence.

Lucky Girls Don't Seek Perfection

In order to attract luck and meet your Lucky Girl Goals, you know you're going to have to be real.

Therefore, there is no room for 'perfect'.

Perfectionism is a trait Lucky Girls need to drop because it's characterised by an unrelenting desire to achieve flawless results, high standards in every endeavour, and being intolerant of mistakes. Perfectionists often set unrealistic standards for themselves and others, and they may be very critical of their own performance.

Perfectionism can be a helpful trait in some cases, and the pursuit of excellence can be commendable, but the relentless need for perfection is not.

There are such things as perfect in life – the perfect sunset, the perfect sandwich, the perfect date, but a perfect life? It's an illusion that often leads to dissatisfaction and links back to a scarcity mindset. Instead, put your attention on accepting life's flaws and finding joy in what lies ahead. Keep in mind that your story is unique to you because of all the ups and downs, difficulties, and victories. So give up trying to be flawless, establish worthwhile objectives, and develop an attitude of thankfulness for the beautifully flawed existence you have.

The Roots Behind Perfectionism:

- **Genetic Basis:** Perfectionism can have a genetic basis with certain personality traits such a conscientiousness and high levels of self-control, predisposing individuals to perfectionist tendencies.

- **Early Life Experiences:** Childhood experiences, including parenting styles and achievement pressure, greatly shape perfectionism. Critical parents and a focus on success can lead to internalising unrealistic standards.

- **Cognitive Factors:** Perfectionists frequently exhibit distorted thinking like all-or-nothing thoughts and catastrophic predictions. These biases drive the pursuit of perfection to avoid failure and criticism.

- **Cultural Expectations:** Competitive societies emphasising achievement and success create intense pressure for perfection. Cultural norms advocating never settling for less can instil the belief that anything other than perfection is unacceptable.

- **Comparison:** Comparing ourselves to external factors, individuals may feel the need to measure up to unrealistic standards set by others, perpetuating the desire for perfection.

Exploring the role of perfectionism in the context of professional athletes, a study by Stoeber in 2015[5] found that athletes with perfectionistic tendencies were more prone to experience performance-related stress and anxiety, leading to decreased enjoyment of their sport.

This is also the case for high achievers; a study of high-achieving students found that their perfectionist tendencies led to an increased fear of failure, reduced self-esteem, and higher levels of stress in academic settings.

Such self-inflicted pressure can create a mental barrier to luck as perfectionists become reluctant to take chances out of fear of failure and not living up to others' expectations. Research conducted by Harvard Business School[6] shows that when individuals perceive others as more successful or accomplished, they may feel hesitant to pursue new ventures or opportunities, fearing they won't measure up. This risk aversion limits the chances of encountering luck through novel experiences and endeavours.

The Debrief: Perfectly Imperfect

This exercise is designed to help you address imperfections by working with compassion.

Reflection

Reflect on a recent situation or experience where you felt frustrated or disappointed due to your perceived imperfection. It could be a mistake you made, a task you didn't complete perfectly, or a flaw you noticed about yourself.

Observation

Imagine stepping outside of yourself and observing the situation as if you were a neutral observer. Try to see the situation from a broader perspective.

As you observe, reaffirm to yourself that everyone makes mistakes and experiences imperfections. It's a natural part of being human.

(continued)

(*continued*)

> ### Recontextualisation
>
> Reflect on the situation from a different angle. Is there a lesson or opportunity for growth that arose from this situation? How might this experience contribute to your personal development? Write down your reflections and observations, and conclude with self-compassionate statements and any perspectives on embracing imperfection.

Lucky Girls Don't Take Life Too Seriously

Life is an intricate journey filled with challenges, successes, and moments of joy. While it is essential to work hard and pursue our goals, getting caught up in the seriousness of life can play havoc with our overall happiness.

There are plenty of times, of course, where we do have to be serious.

If you get a serious medical diagnosis, you're not expected to roll around in fits of giggles or brush it off as if it's a minor inconvenience. Being serious at certain times allows us to fully comprehend and address the gravity of certain situations, make informed decisions, and seek appropriate help or treatment. It is important to find a balance between being serious when necessary and embracing light-heartedness in other aspects of life to maintain overall well-being.

'Lighten up a bit' – not so easy for the introverts in us, but maybe it's something we should try?

If you've seen Disney's *Pocahontas*[7], you may recall Grandmother Willow questioning Pocahontas about marrying a chap back in the village. Pocahontas responded, 'Kocoum? But he's so serious!'

With muscles the size of tree trunks and a stern expression that could scare off a pack of raccoons, Kocoum had a serious case of the grumps.

Meanwhile, Pocahontas, the free-spirited daughter of the chief, found Kocoum to be a bit of an ick and was instead drawn to crazy hot John Smith (a cartoon character, I know) and turned on by his adventurous spirit and captivated by his playful charm.

A bit extreme, but maybe if Kocoum would have just lightened up a bit, cracked a smile once in a while, could laugh at himself, or even joined P on the odd adventure, maybe Pocahontas wouldn't have felt the need to sneak off with John, and maybe Kocoum wouldn't have gotten himself shot and wound up dead.

Without sounding too doom and gloom, note that your physical time on planet Earth is limited. Why waste time being so serious if we're only here for such a short while?

If we spend around one third of our lives asleep (*or at least attempting to*), 92 days on average spent pooping on the toilet, and on average 108 minutes a day scrolling on social media (equating to thumb travelling 52 miles p/a) – with that limited precious time left, do you really want to spend it being a seriously, serious soul?

No – you want your conscious time spent having fun, feeling happy, and full of fulfilment.

It's when we forego fun and get overwhelmed by stress that we inadvertently lose touch with the vitality of life, and in doing so, we compromise the flow of positive energy that affects our luck.

Taylor Swift once stated, 'I don't think you should ever take life so seriously that you forget to play.' Psychology supports the Swifty notion, as playfulness has a positive impact on our emotional and psychological well-being. A study published in the *Journal of Personality and Social Psychology* found that people who exhibit a playful personality tend to experience higher levels of life satisfaction and reduced negative emotions like stress and anxiety. Playfulness has been associated with increased optimism, vitality, and adaptability, enabling individuals to cope more effectively with life's challenges.

Playfulness has long been linked to enhanced creativity and problem-solving abilities. Studying the psychology behind playfulness and children, the *Journal of Experimental Child Psychology*[8] revealed that children engaged in imaginative play demonstrated greater creativity in solving complex tasks. This finding suggests that playfulness stimulates divergent thinking and allows individuals to approach challenges with an open and innovative mindset. Harnessing a playful attitude can unlock the imagination and lead to novel ideas and solutions.

In adulthood, we are uber prone to chronic stress, which can be spearheaded by the fact that we have become more in tune with the severity of life situations. Living in this state of high stress, our adrenals overproduce the stress hormone cortisol, playing havoc with our hormones. On the contrary, engaging in playful activities triggers the release of endorphins, the body's natural stress relievers, and prevents cognitive atrophy from conditions such as Alzheimer's. According to research published in *Perspectives on Psychological Science*, playfulness can serve as a powerful buffer against stress, leading to improved mood and overall well-being. Play provides a much-needed escape from the pressures of daily life, allowing individuals to recharge and rejuvenate. If you've played the computer game *Sims*, you'll know that in order to keep your Sim surviving and thriving, you need to maintain its 'fun metre'. It's the same for us too – we have our own built-in fun metres that need our attention.

We don't need anything to fuel our existing limiting beliefs or inner resistance. When we take life too seriously, it fuels fears and a relentless pursuit of perfection. In contrast, playfulness encourages Lucky Girls to embrace imperfections and approach setbacks with resilience, positively influences how we respond to failure, and boosts our willingness to try again (*hello, growth mindset*).

Founded in 1932, LEGO initially manufactured wooden toys. However, in the 1950s, they began producing their iconic plastic interlocking bricks. Despite facing financial challenges and fierce competition, the company's commitment to playfulness and imagination led to the creation of innovative playsets that captured children's imaginations worldwide. By using a playful approach to product development, LEGO's success demonstrates that you too can be playful in business and life.

'When life throws you a rainy day, play in the puddles.'

Winnie-the-Pooh[9]

We have enough stress, responsibilities, deadlines, or 'rain' to deal with in our day. Like with the quote from Pooh bear, if we can learn to stop being so serious and add a little playfulness, we will experience greater daily satisfaction. Life is a grand adventure, and by infusing play, you can discover joy in the simplest of moments.

The Debrief: It's Playtime, Kids

How to have a little laugh:

Be who you are when you're around your bestie

When around the people closest to us, we tend to be our strange, weird, vulnerable, and fun versions of ourselves. When I'm with my bestie, we effortlessly transition from deep discussions about life, politics, and the planet, to far less grown-up antics with our unhinged impressions and crazy cackling. We know we can speak openly about the dark times we experience, just as we can be silly and celebrate the funny stories in our day.

Use that same energy that you have with your bestie and let it pour out into other areas of your life, balancing the serious with the silliness.

Allow your body to play

Practising playful embodiment is a good way to get out of your head. Move through your own yoga flow with your favourite tunes. Dance and sing. Walk in the grass barefoot. Get the Lego out or a board game. Whatever you do, make time for playtime.

Laugh at yourself

Cultivate the ability to laugh at your own mistakes and idiosyncrasies. See that nobody is perfect, and laughter can be a powerful tool for self-acceptance and growth.

(continued)

(*continued*)

Connect with your inner child

Reconnect with the playful and carefree spirit of your inner child. Inner Child work is often perceived as quite deep, especially if you did have a traumatic childhood. A light approach to connecting with your inner child is to engage in activities you loved as a child, or give them a chance to do something they always wanted but couldn't. Relish any sense of nostalgia and create joy for your inner child.

Thoughts and Reflections

In this chapter, we've explored the traits that Lucky Girls consciously distance themselves from, recognising them as potential roadblocks on the journey to a more fortunate and enriching existence. These traits, if left unchecked, have the power to undermine our progress, erode self-worth, strain connections with others, and plunge us into negativity. It's crucial to understand that these guidelines are not rigid laws dictating the presence or absence of luck in our lives; rather, they are guideposts, offering direction as we navigate our paths.

Luck isn't an all-or-nothing phenomenon, and this chapter is not about coercing you into a predetermined mould. Your uniqueness is celebrated here, and we aim to preserve your individuality. Instead, view these insights as opportunities for personal growth. By identifying, addressing, and evolving beyond these traits, you open the door for luck to seamlessly integrate into your life. This transformation will allow your true self to shine outwardly, shaping your experiences in profound and positive ways. Embrace this journey of self-discovery, for it is the key to unlocking a more fortunate and fulfilling life.

6

Lucky Girls Do This . . .

Having explored the traits Lucky Girls lack, let's now shift our focus and investigate the traits that Lucky Girls do possess, which contribute to their ability to live a charmed life. By gently incorporating some of the techniques outlined in this chapter, you can embrace the essence of a Lucky Girl and set the stage for attracting luck into your own life.

Before you continue reading, take a moment to revisit the Lucky Girl you analysed in Chapter 3. Recall their unique and wonderful traits. It's likely that these fortunate individuals have utilised at least one of the techniques outlined in this chapter at some point.

There is an old saying that goes *'You become what you admire'*. This adage emphasises the importance of embodying the traits of someone that you admire, so you can be more like them and able to attract easier. The whole idea behind this saying is rooted in the belief that we are attracted to people who possess the qualities that we would like to have ourselves. Therefore, by emulating such admirable traits, we take a step towards our Lucky Girl Goals.

Be mindful of the traits we emulate, as these traits tend to have an impact on our overall well-being. Psychologists suggest that mimicking the behaviours of individuals who embody traits we admire can improve our mood and increase our self-esteem. By embodying these qualities, we can feel more confident in ourselves, which is again vital to achieving our goals.

This sentiment is supported by a study conducted by psychologists at the University of Hertfordshire, which found that individuals have a better self-image when they adopt traits they admire.[1]

Note that this isn't about transforming yourself into a copycat version of someone else. You can still remain authentically you. By incorporating a few drops of Lucky Girl essence, you're enhancing the very best version of yourself.

Your uniqueness is your strength; your messy and ridiculous aspects are what make you pure and beautiful. By adopting just one of the exercises below, you accelerate your luck. While the list may appear lengthy and initially overwhelming, breaking it down and taking your time with each exercise will make the process more manageable.

Perhaps life has led you to feel a bit like a miserable old witch, and right now, you might identify more with the traits listed in 'Lucky Girls Don't do this'. However, be assured that the essence of being a Lucky Girl is already within you. The tools presented below will simply provide a helping hand to tap into those inherent powers.

So without further ado, Lucky Girls do this . . .

Lucky Girls Answer the Daily Questions

A significant practice Lucky Girls undertake is the capacity for daily journaling.

Ask any therapist, and I bet they will strongly recommend journaling as a valuable tool to enhance your emotional and mental well-being. Many renowned experts and practitioners in the field firmly believe that consistent journaling can lead to profound self-discovery and growth.

Journaling will be your best friend when it comes to your Lucky Girl life:

- You unpack your core values.

- You check-in with yourself and acknowledge how you *really* feel.

- You track your progress.

- You celebrate the milestones.

One of the main benefits is its ability to reduce stress and anxiety levels. A 2018 study published in the journal

Anxiety, Stress, & Coping found that journaling for just 15 minutes a day for three days a week was effective in reducing anxiety symptoms in people with generalised anxiety disorder.[2]

This reduction in negative emotions can help individuals focus on more positive thoughts and emotions, thereby attracting more positive experiences into their lives.

By putting thoughts and emotions down on paper, you gain further understanding and perspective on your problems and find healthy ways to cope and reframe when faced with life's stressors.

Not only a great quick win for calm, but it also assists in cultivating a positive mindset in the long term. By writing our thoughts down, we can notice thought patterns and work from shifting from negative to positive. When we experience positive emotions, it increases our creativity, expands our horizons, and acts as a driving force, pushing us to take action towards our goals.

Journaling facilitates Lucky Girl Syndrome, as it allows us to become more self-aware, understand our experiences on a deeper level, and become more mindful. Writing down thoughts, feelings, behaviours, and emotions provides an opportunity to reflect on what may be your strengths and weaknesses and helps peek into patterns in your mind and behaviours. With that, we can identify areas where we might be holding ourselves back, see common thought patterns form and provide rationales. See journaling as qualitative data capture, where you can spot key themes to then add to your limiting beliefs chart too.

It is this increased self-awareness that will lead us to greater emotional intelligence, better decision-making, and improved relationships with others.

Writing down and answering the daily questions, helps facilitate your luck, as we are able to clearly visualise the outcome we desire and set intentions for our day so we can bring about positive change.

The University of Carolina studied this notion of journaling and manifesting. They concluded that those who wrote about their positive experiences and visualised positive outcomes for just five minutes a day found themselves in better moods and less stressed. By reinforcing positive thoughts and intentions through daily journaling, we create a positive mindset that attracts positive outcomes.[3]

Answering the daily questions helps us shape our experiences. By writing down our plans and aspirations, we are more likely to achieve our objectives. Gail Matthews, a psychology professor at Dominican University, California, conducted a study that found that individuals who wrote down their goals achieved a 42% higher success rate than those who didn't.[4] With a statistic like that, surely, it's worth a try?

To get the most out of daily journaling as a tool for Lucky Girl Syndrome, just let your pen flow. Set aside time each day to sit quietly, ideally in the morning to set yourself up for the day ahead, and just check in with yourself, writing whatever pops into your mind or questioning your feelings more. At first, it may seem time-consuming, but it doesn't have to be an essay, and you aren't getting marked on it. A few brief lines will even do, and it's up to you how brief or detailed you want to keep it. It's your personal private time, so just be.

Putting pen to paper, let your daydreams run wild, and as you do so, imagine yourself reaching your goals. Allow journaling to help you track your progress, and when you read back, reflect on how far you've come and reinforce that positive mindset to keep going – the 'celebrate' aspect!

Journaling is one of the most successful well-being tools out there – it's easily accessible (you just need a pen and paper), incredibly effective, and free!

The Debrief: The Daily Questions . . .

Use the prompts and questions below to act as a guide – clarify your goals, set your intention, shift your mindset, and have yourself a beautiful, lucky day!

You don't have to answer them all, just pick at least one to start your day. Allow for the process to be flexible and customisable to suit your preferences.

1. How am I feeling this morning?

2. What are the top three things that I am grateful for in my life right now?

3. What are the three main tasks I need to do today?

4. What small steps can I take today towards my Lucky Girl Goals?

5. What do I need to let go of in order to have a great day?

6. How can I show up as my best possible self today?

7. What's one thing I can do today to get outside my comfort zone?

8. How will I prioritise self-care today?

9. What can I do for someone else that will bring them happiness?

10. What affirmation can I take with me today?

Lucky Girls Are Curious

Question everything in life.

In a world inundated with information and ideas, it becomes increasingly crucial for us to question everything, particularly when it comes to concepts like the law of attraction and Lucky Girl Syndrome. Creating a balance between a critical mindset and an optimistic sense of curiosity allows us to evaluate beliefs and theories and set our goals thoughtfully, ensuring that they are based on sound reasoning. Explore answers to your questions with open inquiry, so you can navigate through the vast sea of information and make informed decisions about where and how we can start to get lucky.

One of the personal characteristics of Lucky Girls is that they are courageously curious and openly optimistic. Maybe irritatingly so, but optimism 'is faith that leads to achievement' (Helen Keller).

Think back to when you were just a small child and how exciting the world used to be. Hearing a bee buzzing, smelling a freshly baked cookie, seeing a fluffy dog walk past – we would be in total awe, and all such curious beings . . . what happened?!

Never-ending to-do lists, life stressors, deadlines, and countless emails are what happened, and the buzzing we now notice is our phone notifications going off, telling us of something else we have to do.

Now that we have become better aligned and more self-aware, connecting back to curiosity should be an easy transition.

It's all about expanding your range: you become encouraged to explore and try new things, pushing you outside your comfort zone and tackling unfamiliar situations with confidence.

When we get curious, old judgements fall away. Preconceived notions and biases are challenged, and it urges you to question your beliefs and see things from different perspectives. By keeping curious, you gain a broader understanding of complex issues and become more open-minded and adaptable to change. As you continuously question and learn, you become more flexible in your mindset and better equipped to problem solve.

It may not come as naturally as it once did when we were kids, so we have to add it to our daily routines. The more you are curious, the easier it will become, and eventually be a natural habit once more. Re-awaken your child-like self, broaden your experiences, and look at the world from a new and profound sense of appreciation for the diverse and ever-changing aspects of life.

The Debrief: Act Alien

Go about your day acting as if you are an alien who's just landed on planet Earth.

Imagine yourself experiencing everything an alien would for the first time, appreciating every aspect – hearing the birds chirp, smelling the rich aroma of your morning coffee, feeling the weight of the clothes on your body, seeing a person smile.

(continued)

(continued)

Pretend you know nothing about the tasks you currently do and keep curious – driving your car, the project you're working on, the organisation you may be working for, etc. Examine each situation and interaction. Pretend to know zero about these weird creatures called humans or what happens on this planet. You are here to learn as much as possible about these interesting and beautiful things, seeing it all in a new light. Develop a sincere appreciation.

Lucky Girls Harness the Power of Affirmations

Just like Marmite – love them or hate them, affirmations are a quintessential aspect of being a Lucky Girl.

Affirmations can be such an easy, transformative tool to quickly switch up our vibes and change up our negative thought patterns and replace them with constructive, optimistic ones.

And no, that self-help guru you follow on Instagram was not the founding father of affirmations. The origins of affirmations can be traced back to ancient civilizations, their rich history goes back thousands of years, stemming from the ancient Hindus and Buddhists, who used mantra meditation as a way to quiet the mind and focus on higher truths. Years later in the West, French philosopher René Descartes was the first recorded to use affirmations; famously stating 'Cogito, ergo sum' or 'I think, therefore I am'.

Fast forward to the nineteenth century, affirmations became popular in The New Thought movement, which based its ideations on how positive thinking creates positive results in life. One of the early leaders of the movement, Phineas Quimby, developed a method of using affirmative statements to help his patients overcome their illnesses. Mary Baker Eddy, the founder of Christian Science, could also be argued to be the Founding Mother of Affirmations. Eddy developed the current notion further, penning a book called *Science and Health with Key to the Scriptures*, which detailed how she healed herself from various injuries and illnesses and contained positive statements to be used for personal affirmation.

If you've read twentieth-century Napoleon Hill's classic book *Think and Grow Rich*, you'll see even back then, this line of thinking transformed people's lives.

In more recent times, the self-help movement has popularised the practice of affirmations, which is used by millions around the world for personal transformation and as way to achieve success and attract luck.

We really have no full idea of the extent that our thoughts and words can shape our reality.

Affirmations affirm our thoughts.

Combining affirmations with a desire to attract more luck is an easy yet effective way to help you meet your goals. The key is to consistently repeat your affirmations, and over time they will become an ingrained part of your natural thought process. Just like brushing your teeth twice a day, make them a daily habit.

As the Law of Attraction posits that our thoughts and emotions attract corresponding experiences into our lives, affirmations align perfectly with this universal law as they enable us to focus our thoughts on what we want to manifest, thereby attracting those experiences into our reality. Intentionally repeating positive affirmations, you can shift your vibrational frequency to match the desired outcomes, thus facilitating the manifestation process.

There is a ton of empirical research investigating the effects of affirmations in various domains. A study by the University of Texas demonstrated that engaging in self-affirmation exercises can have significant positive effects.[5] It helps reduce defensiveness, promotes open-mindedness, and encourages positive behaviour change. Furthermore, self-affirmation appears to have stress-buffering effects, leading to improved well-being and better coping with challenging situations.

Self-affirmation techniques can significantly reduce the effects of cognitive dissonance and enhance problem-solving abilities.[6] Another study published in *Psychological Science* demonstrated that self-affirmations could buffer against the negative effects of stress and improve performance under pressure.[7]

These findings underscore the potential for affirmations to influence our mental game and manage our mindset.

Serena Williams, one of the most accomplished tennis players of all time, is known for using affirmations to boost her confidence and focus on the court. She often speaks positive statements to herself before and during matches, reinforcing her belief in her abilities and staying resilient during challenging moments.

Even Queen B talks frequently about using affirmations to stay grounded and maintain her self-belief, which radiates outward through her lyrics, her extreme confidence, and her powerful stage presence.

Take your affirmations anywhere and everywhere with you. Change your wallpaper, set reminders, and say them when you look into the mirror. Play them on your hot girl walk or while driving your car – wherever you are, let affirmations guide you to greatness.

The best? You can literally drum up an affirmation for anything. In the back of the book, you'll find a selection of Lucky Girl Affirmations or why not have a go at making your own?

The Debrief: Your Lucky Girl Affirmations

To really harness the full effect of Lucky Girl Affirmations, craft them in a way that resonates with your subconscious mind. Consider the following key principles:

- **Use the present tense:** Phrase your LGA in the present tense, as if the desired outcome is already manifesting. This helps to align your subconscious mind with the belief that your desire is already a reality.

    For example: 'I am so lucky'

- **Focus on the positive:** Focus on the positive and affirm what you want, rather than what you want to avoid.

    When I first read *The Secret*, I realised I had been doing this so wrong. Rhonda Byrne suggests instead of saying the opposite of what you want, e.g. 'I want no drama', switch this to 'I attract peaceful exchanges with all I interact with', or instead of saying 'I am anti-war' switch to 'I am pro-peace'.

- **Be clear:** Like your Lucky Girl Goals, your affirmations require you to be specific about the outcome you desire. The more clarity, the more you will attract the essence of the affirmation.

- **Invoke emotion:** Emotions amplify the impact of affirmations. Infuse your affirmations with excitement to enhance their vibrational frequency and resonance.

- **Rinse & repeat:** Consistency is key when using affirmations. Repeat them daily, perhaps after your morning daily questions. Like with your Lucky Girl Goals Guide, place them somewhere at the forefront so you can easily repeat them yourself multiple times throughout the day to fully reinforce your Lucky intentions.

Lucky Girls Tap

Don't worry, you're not going to be asked to learn how to tap dance here; just learn how to EFT Tap.

The Emotional Freedom Technique is a therapeutic approach, backed by science, that works via the body's energy system to eliminate negative emotions or traumatic past events.

This effective technique involves applying gentle percussive tapping on the meridian points located on the energy channels that run through your body.

Through stimulating the meridian points by tapping, you access the body's energy, which sends signals to the amygdala in your brain to control your level of stress, thus reducing the intensity of the negative emotion from your issue and restoring balance to your disturbed energy.

As part of neuro-linguistic programming, we use the voice to help rewire the brain and unravel negative thought patterns. By releasing the negative emotions through EFT, we rebalance the nervous system in a non-invasive way and take away the emotional charge, enabling you to move on from trauma, once and for all . . .

The EFT technique is used far and wide to aid people in their healing process. Clients include those struggling with issues ranging from anxiety to depression, to weight issues right down to post-traumatic stress disorder.

Here's how EFT can help you get lucky:

- **Clearing Limiting Beliefs:** EFT involves tapping on specific acupuncture points while focusing on negative emotions or beliefs. By doing so, you can release and clear out limiting beliefs that might be holding you back from believing in your ability to manifest luck. For example, if you hold a subconscious belief that you're not deserving of good things happening to you, EFT can help you reframe and release that belief, allowing you to be more open to receiving luck and abundance.

- **Reducing Emotional Blocks:** Negative emotions such as fear, doubt, and anxiety can create energetic blocks that impede the flow of positive energy and opportunities into your life. EFT can help you process and release these emotions, allowing you to create a more positive and receptive energetic state that aligns with your manifestation goals.

- **Enhancing Positive Mindset:** EFT uses positive affirmations during tapping to reprogramme your subconscious mind in alignment with your manifesting goals. By focusing on luck, abundance, and positive outcomes, this technique promotes a more positive and optimistic mindset.

- **Aligning with Gratitude:** EFT can be used to enhance your sense of gratitude by tapping while focusing on things you're grateful for, maintaining a positive vibration, essential for manifesting.

- **Releasing Resistance:** Resistance to change or fear of the unknown can impact manifestation. EFT identifies and releases this resistance by addressing underlying emotions, clearing the way for luck and opportunities to manifest.

EFT is a tool that works best when used consistently. Over time, it can complement your overall manifestation practises by helping you clear away emotional blocks and align your energy with the positive outcomes you seek.

The Debrief: Tapping into Luck

Download your free EFT guide on the website (https://lucky-collective.com/) and try out EFT meditation audio or tapping scripts to align yourself with the energy of luck.

Lucky Girls Love Lucid Dreaming

Visualise your highest self and start showing up as that person.

Sometimes, your mind doesn't actually know the difference between imagination and reality.

OK, this sounds very delulu, but dreaming in all forms is quite remarkable.

Let's explore a quick exercise together:

Let your mind wander as you daydream, imagining yourself biting into a juicy, tangy lemon.

Now, be honest with yourself – can you feel a hint of saliva forming in your mouth? This simple demonstration illustrates that our mind has an extraordinary capacity to respond to vivid mental imagery, blurring the lines between what's imagined and what's real.

So if you can imagine biting into a lemon and getting that reaction, what do you think will happen when you manage to visualise getting what you want and triggering positive neurochemicals in the brain like serotonin – by just imagining being lucky?

Thanks to research proving it so, we contemplate our future twice as much as our past, offering numerous advantages if approached realistically. Through visualisation, strategising, planning, and preparation, we can explore various possibilities and pathways.

Just like Sleepy Jean herself, I'm a daydream believer and always have been. When I was in school, I used to love the classroom, especially when sat by a window, because it was my ultimate daydreaming time (classic ADHD symptom). I did it so much that I would either get into a lot of trouble, or teachers would simply ignore me as they couldn't get through to me. There would often be the snapping of fingers and the occasional book slamming on my desk to snap me back into the current reality (*who honestly cares about equations anyway?!*) but I genuinely couldn't help it!

It's no wonder that even now in my adulthood, I'm still an avid daydreamer and visualiser, and even like to control the dreams in my sleep state to influence what I want.

You can too, Lucky Girl, with Lucid Dreaming.

The realm of dreams has long captivated human imagination, offering a canvas for the subconscious mind to paint its intricacies of thoughts, emotions, and experiences. Within this enigmatic domain lies a phenomenon known as lucid dreaming, a state where dreamers become aware of their dream while immersed in it. As the boundaries between reality and imagination blur, the concept of lucid dreaming has gained attention not only for its psychological significance but also for its potential in the realm of manifestation.

Research has shown that visualisation, a key component of Lucky Girl Syndrome and manifestation, activates brain regions similar to those engaged during actual experiences.[8] Lucid dreaming offers a heightened platform for visualisation, allowing dreamers to create vivid mental scenarios and immerse themselves in their aspirations. In a study by Schredl and Erlacher, it was found that individuals who practised visualisation techniques within lucid dreams reported enhanced feelings of self-efficacy and a more positive outlook.[9]

Furthermore, lucid dreaming serves as an experiential playground for practising desired behaviours. By simulating success scenarios in dreams, dreamers engage in a form of rehearsal that can boost their confidence and competence in real-life situations. This aligns with studies on motor skill acquisition, where mental practice has been shown to enhance actual performance.[10] Lucid dreaming, therefore, becomes a sanctuary for risk-free exploration, allowing individuals to refine their approach and skills before confronting challenges in the waking world.

As emotions are all important in the manifestation process, with positive emotions acting as catalysts for aligning with desired outcomes,[11] lucid dreaming provides a platform for amplifying these emotions, allowing dreamers to experience the joy, excitement, and fulfilment of having manifested their goals. As dreamers interact with dream environments, they can actively evoke and intensify positive emotions associated with their aspirations, leading to an emotional alignment that can transcend into their waking lives.

Lucid dreaming also holds the potential to dismantle limiting beliefs that hinder manifestation efforts. Within the dream realm, the mind can confront deep-seated fears or doubts and, through conscious interaction with dream elements, initiate cognitive restructuring. This aligns with research in cognitive behavioural therapy, which emphasises the importance of identifying and challenging irrational beliefs.[12] The introspective nature of lucid dreaming serves as a therapeutic avenue for dismantling psychological barriers that impede progress.

Studies have demonstrated that intentions and beliefs influence the content of dreams.[13] In a lucid dream, the dreamer's focused intention can shape the dream narrative, amplifying the influence of thought and emotion. This phenomenon aligns with research on focused attention and its impact on dream experiences.[14] By consciously directing energy and intention within a lucid dream, you can tap into a unique dimension of manifestation, where thoughts and emotions merge to sculpt dreamscapes reflective of their desires.

The nexus between lucid dreaming and Lucky Girl Syndrome presents a frontier of untapped potential. Your blanket of dreams offers an expansive realm for visualisation and experiential practice, emotional alignment, belief restructuring, and intentional direction. While research on the direct link between lucid dreaming and manifestation is limited, existing studies on visualisation, cognitive restructuring, emotional regulation, and dream content offer compelling insights into the symbiotic relationship between the two phenomena. As science continues to unveil the intricacies of consciousness and dreams, Lucky Girls keen on manifesting aspirations may find the key to unlocking creative potential lies within the realm of lucid dreaming.

The Debrief: Lucky Dreams

To begin, set a clear intention for your dream, visualise what luck looks like, and clear your mind through techniques like EFT tapping, meditations, grounding breaths, progressive muscle relaxation, or affirmations. Visualise yourself experiencing the scenario you intend to manifest, feeling excitement and gratitude. As you fall asleep, keep your intention and visualisation in mind, maintaining awareness. Once lucid, stay calm and focused, using lucidity to manifest the desired luck. Explore the dream world with intention and ask for guidance from dream characters. Generate positivity while in the dream, as it aligns with your intention and enhances the manifestation process. Once you wake up, jot down any dreams, details, emotions, and insights to enhance dream recall and connection to the dream world. This will help to reinforce the balance between your conscious and subconscious mind.

Lucky Girls Are Kind

Human kindness has always been present in society, whether in the form of religious and/or spiritual beliefs or as social norms and expectations. Religions, while they disagree on some points, all consider human kindness to be a core value in their ancient texts.

Kindness, the delightful act of showing compassion, consideration, and goodwill towards others, is a fundamental virtue that has the ability to create positive ripples in our lives and the world around us. Beyond its inherent moral value, kindness is also closely intertwined with any of the laws of manifestation, and to be a Lucky Girl, you have to be a **Lovely Girl.**

We are all well within our rights to ask the universe for more wealth, success, and power. However, if we really want to attract these things, we've got to bring kindness, front and centre; kindness to ourselves, to each other, to our community, and to the wider world – even to the people that we strongly believe don't deserve it.

Kindness is key.

Empirical research supports the transformative effects of kindness on both individuals and communities. A study published in *The Journal of Social Psychology* demonstrated that performing acts of kindness can lead to a significant increase in subjective well-being, happiness, and life satisfaction.[15] A further study conducted by the University of California, revealed that individuals who engage in acts of kindness experience a boost in their sense of connection and positive social relationships.[16] These findings highlight the profound impact of kindness on personal well-being and social cohesion.

Not only do we need to be kind, but we also need to look for and focus on the kindness around us. If it's not bang right in front of you, widen your lens slightly, and you'll see – as in Hugh Grant's closing line in the movie *Love Actually* –'Love, actually, is all around'.[17]

When you give out kindness, you become aligned. When you are aligned, you create a more harmonious and interconnected world – one that works with you, not against you. One that attracts luck.

Kindness and luck coexist due to:

- **Positive Energy:** Acts of kindness generate positive energy and vibrations, elevating our overall vibrational frequency. This positive energy resonates with similar frequencies in the universe, facilitating the manifestation process.

- **Rewires the brain:** Acts of kindness release both endorphins and oxytocin (our happy hormones) and create new neural connections. The implications of such plasticity in the brain are that altruism and kindness become self-reinforcing habits, requiring less and less effort to exercise.

- **Gratitude and Abundance:** Kindness cultivates gratitude and an abundance mindset, which are essential elements of successful manifestation. By acknowledging and appreciating the abundance in our lives, we attract more positive experiences and opportunities.

- **Social Connections:** These relationships provide support, encouragement, and collaboration, further enhancing our ability to manifest our goals and desires.

- **Ripple Effect:** Kindness has a ripple effect, spreading positivity and inspiring others to engage in acts of kindness. As we contribute to a kinder world, the collective consciousness is elevated, aligning us with a higher vibrational frequency conducive to manifestation.

'In a world where you can be anything, be kind.'

We can all make a commitment to be kind if we wish. The beauty of it all – it's free, easy to implement, and open to anyone. Accessible to the rich and the poor, and is a universally spoken language.

Embrace kindness as a transformative practice, recognising that here and now it is a force that generates good, joy, positivity, and a profound impact on the world we co-create but also enriches your quality of life. Send those ripples outward and facilitate their constructive pursuit. When you embrace kindness in all its glory, don't be surprised by how sudden the positive impact is and the power your luck attracts.

Contribute to a collective positive consciousness by aligning with frequencies for successful manifestation – simply by being kind. Amidst all discussed in this book, if you only adopt one thing, let it be kindness.

The Debrief: Loving Kindness

Take a moment to send loving vibes to yourself and then extend those vibes out to a loved one, an acquaintance, someone challenging and then everyone else in the world. On the website (https://lucky-collective.com/) you'll find a guided Lucky Girl Loving Kindness Meditation (LGLKM), which directs your focus towards kindness and generates compassion.

Lucky Girls Have an Attitude of Gratitude

A common theme you will find in most chapters of this book and any text on manifesting is the power of gratitude.

Even if you are not well-versed in the laws of manifestation, it's basic manners to be thankful and practise gratitude.

The art of gratitude is more than a mere thank you. Gratitude is an enlightening emotion that can have a significant impact on our mental and emotional well-being. It is the act of acknowledging and appreciating the good things in our lives, no matter how big or small.

Adopting an attitude of gratitude is essential for manifesting your desires and should ideally be a pivotal part of your Lucky Girl day.

Lucky Girls are **Gracious Girls**!

The warm feeling of thankfulness and appreciation is far more than a social gesture. Dr Joe Dispenza says, gratitude is the ultimate state of receivership.

And it's so true. Whenever we feel a sense of gratitude, no matter how big or small, we release one of the most positive and highest frequencies there are. And then guess what? When we are in a state of gratitude, we can attract the things we want into our lives easier.

When we practise gratitude, we send out those all-encompassing, beaming rays of positivity out into the universe. This positive energy, as we know, attracts more positive things into our lives, leading to more abundance, joy, success, luck, or whatever you want to call it. Be so damn grateful that these beaming rays of positivity shine out from every cell in your body.

At its heart, gratitude works with the brain's reward system, a complex network that reinforces positive behaviours and emotions. This system is responsible for experiencing pleasure and motivation, encouraging us to repeat actions that are beneficial to our well-being. Gratitude activates the reward circuitry, creating a reinforcing loop that encourages us to express appreciation and maintain social bonds.

Happy hormones have been mentioned previously, and with gratitude, these happy hormones hone in. Scientific studies on this topic have all concluded that when we feel grateful, the brain releases dopamine, a neurotransmitter associated with pleasure and reward. This surge of dopamine makes us feel good and encourages us to seek out similar experiences in the future. As a result, expressing gratitude becomes a natural and rewarding behaviour.

In addition to dopamine, another neurotransmitter, serotonin, increases when we feel grateful too. The interaction between dopamine and serotonin in the brain creates a powerful synergy, reinforcing the emotional rewards associated with gratitude.

This biochemical interplay enhances the likelihood of gratitude becoming a habit, leading individuals to engage in more prosocial behaviours and strengthen social connections.

Brain imaging studies, such as functional magnetic resonance imaging (fMRI) and positron emission tomography (PET), have provided valuable insights into how gratitude impacts neural activity. These studies reveal that when individuals experience gratitude, specific brain regions light up, indicating heightened activity.

One brain region that consistently shows increased activation during expressions of gratitude is the anterior cingulate cortex (ACC). The ACC is associated with processing emotions and regulating social behaviour. Its involvement in gratitude suggests that this emotion helps maintain social bonds and prosocial behaviour.

The prefrontal cortex (PFC), a region located at the front of the brain, is responsible for high-order cognitive functions, including decision-making, social skills, and emotional regulation. Science has linked gratitude to increased activity in the PFC, indicating that expressing gratitude may enhance cognitive processes related to social interactions and emotional well-being.

When we practise gratitude, our brains flood with the good.

When we experience the good, our outlook remains positive.

This positivity generated by gratitude works in all areas of our lives. It's a boost to our mental health, and even our physical health gets impacted. Did you know grateful people tend to have fewer aches and pains, better sleep, and stronger immune systems?!

Participants in these studies reported reduced symptoms of depression and anxiety, as well as enhanced immune system functioning. The act of focusing on gratitude helps shift attention away from negative thoughts and stressors, promoting mental and physical resilience.

Can't find a single reason to be grateful? NONSENSE.

Put the book down and take a look around you. Step outside of your own perspective, and you'll undoubtedly discover numerous reasons to feel thankful. Gratitude often lies in the simplest things – the sun shining, a smile from a stranger, the air you breathe. Expand your awareness beyond your immediate concerns, and you'll find a world full of blessings waiting to be acknowledged.

The Debrief: Attitude of Gratitude

- **Keep a gratitude journal:** Each evening, fill a page in your journal listing all that you are grateful for and what gave you joy that day.

- **Write a thank you note:** Gratitude letter writing is a heartfelt practice that involves expressing appreciation to people who have positively impacted your life. This intervention not only enhances the well-being of the sender but also strengthens social connections.

- **Say thanks:** Expressing gratitude through words is a powerful way to practise gratitude. Make a habit of saying thank you to the people in your life for the things that they do for you.

Lucky Girls Use Lucky Charms

Will a four-leaf clover fix all your problems? *Probably not.*

Will the meaning or ritual behind it help you create more luck? **Yes.**

No, I've not gone totally crazy in writing the final few chapters of this book; let me explain . . .

I'll admit I'm a little superstitious – not to the point where I poo-poo the whole notion of lucky props, nor to the point where I have to immediately cross a road when I see a black cat – but there is a method to the madness when it comes to lucky charms.

Humans have been employing superstitions for centuries in an attempt to call in luck.

I once had a friend who had a 'lucky vibrator'. This would make me think two lines of thoughts:

1. How can a vibrator be lucky?

2. How many vibrators does she have to be able to say that this particular one is lucky?

Putting aside my questions about her vibrator collection, I quizzed her on the lucky aspect:

'If I use it in the morning ahead of what I thought would be a stressful day ahead, I would find it would actually turn out to be a very good one!' Amazed and in awe she has time to masturbate in the morning, I was also intrigued by the belief that an item could bring such good fortune.

And she's not alone – over one third of Brits are said to even own a lucky pair of pants!

Mecca Bingo, a UK-based gambling company, conducted a survey on 'How superstitious is the UK?'[18] They found that one fifth of Brits believe following superstitions will help ward off bad luck, with a further third relying on lucky charms to bring them success.

The study by Mecca Bingo also found that Britons are certainly not willing to risk it when it comes to something that may affect their luck, with nearly 40 per cent of the UK admitting superstitions are unlikely to come to anything, but they carry the rituals out anyway.

When it comes to Brits' superstitions and believing we can control our own luck, the following lucky charms come up top: socks (36%), pants (35%), coins (23%), toys (12%), and a statue of a Buddha (11%).

For the critics amongst us, there is no scientific evidence to support the efficacy of charms, rituals, or lucky symbols; however, there is evidence suggesting these practices persist due to the psychological comfort they provide.

Lucky charms and superstitions can give us a sense of control over uncertain situations, reducing anxiety and increasing confidence. According to the professionals, there is absolutely nothing wrong with having small traditions or sentimental symbols to make you feel luckier. Rituals such as wearing your lucky pair of knickers or carrying a lucky crystal in your bra help us feel more competent, connected, and protected, and reinforce our beliefs in luck.

A Charming History

Going back through the history books, we can see that humans have always sought to use various methods to attract luck and good fortune into their lives in the form of rituals and objects. One such approach is the use of props, including tokens, amulets, talismans, crystals, lucky charms, and superstitious objects. These props are believed to possess energetic qualities that can influence the flow of luck and create positive vibrations in our surroundings. They are also believed to carry the favour of deities, providing protection, prosperity, and success.

Culturally, charms have been woven into the fabric of traditions and folklore. For instance, horseshoes are believed to bring luck due to their resemblance to the crescent moon, a symbol of fertility and protection in many cultures. In Irish folklore, finding a rare four-leaf clover is considered a stroke of luck, as each leaf represents hope, faith, love, and luck. These symbols transcend time and place, connecting generations through shared beliefs in the power of these objects to attract positive outcomes.

Even in the modern day, props still hold both psychological and symbolic significance, serving as tangible representations of our intentions, beliefs, and desires. These objects have the power to influence our mindset and perception of luck. By possessing and interacting with them, we tap into a deeper psychological connection with our goals, adding to a positive outlook and enhancing our belief in attracting good fortune. The symbolism embedded in these objects creates a bridge between our inner thoughts and the external world, shaping our perception of luck and reinforcing our sense of agency in manifesting positive outcomes.

Scientific research may not fully support the energetic claims, but our belief in objects' luck-enhancing abilities may trigger the placebo effect. This psychological and physiological response works with anticipation of positive outcomes, amplifying experiences of luck. Personalised significance transforms objects into reflections of values and aspirations. For instance, a treasured heirloom necklace carries sentimental value, evoking positive emotions and gratitude. Similarly, students or athletes may rely on specific items for luck during exams or competitions, leveraging psychological associations. These items show that luck perception is influenced by mentality and intention rather than just chance, establishing a concrete connection between beliefs and psychological empowerment and affording the chance to alter reality and draw in favourable outcomes.

The psychology behind superstitious beliefs reveals how our minds can be powerful allies in attracting luck. When we believe in the positive effects of a lucky charm, we unconsciously shape our mindset to be open to possibilities and opportunities. This mindset, in turn, affects our behaviour and decisions, increasing our chances of experiencing favourable outcomes. It's a positive form of self-fulfilling prophecy that illustrates the intricate relationship between belief, perception, and reality.

Woo-woo or not, lucky charms could hold one of the keys to unlocking the door to luck.

Lucky Rituals

Rituals are not mere routines; they are profound expressions of our beliefs and desires. Crafting rituals that incorporate lucky charms transforms the mundane into the extraordinary and is an invitation to live with intention and purpose. Luck charms heighten your senses, awareness, and presence. As you engage with these symbols, become attuned to their energy and the intentions they represent. These interactions deepen your connection to the present moment, allowing you to infuse even the smallest of tasks with purpose and intentionality.

By intertwining the tangible with the intangible, you tap into the transformative potential of these rituals, inviting luck and positive energy to flow into your life. A ritual can be a small gesture such as using sage to clear negative energy from your home or burning incense, to a full-blown spiritual practice banishing the juju, but we Lucky Girls like to keep things simple.

May the exploration of props and their symbolic power bring you closer to aligning with the flow of luck and manifesting positive experiences in your life. Embrace the potency of intention, belief, and positive energy as you seamlessly integrate these props into your routine.

The Debrief: Lucky Girls' Lucky Charms

Let this ritual create a channel for attracting abundant luck and positive outcomes into your life.

- **Lucky Charm:** Choose a lucky charm that resonates with you, holds positive energy, and aligns with your intention. It could be a crystal that symbolises abundance, a small object with personal significance, or a traditional lucky symbol like a horseshoe or a four-leaf clover.

- **Cleanse and Charge:** Before incorporating the charm into your ritual, cleanse it of any residual energies it may carry. You can do this by gently rinsing it under running water or placing it in sunlight for a few hours. As you do so, visualise the charm absorbing pure and positive energy.

- **Choose a Meaningful Time:** Select a specific time for your ritual. This could be the beginning of your day, a significant date, full or new moon or a time when you feel particularly connected to your intentions.

- **Sacred Space:** Light a candle or some incense to create a soothing ambience. Place the charm in front of you, allowing it to become the focal point of your intention.

- **Express:** Hold the charm, speak aloud or silently your intention for attracting more luck into your desired area of life. Use positive and affirming language as if your intention has already manifested.

- **Infuse with Energy:** Imagine radiant, golden light surrounding the charm, infusing it with the energy of luck and abundance. Feel the

(continued)

(continued)

> positive vibrations emanating from the charm,
> resonating with your desires. Meditate, tap, or
> just simply breathe as you sit with both your
> charm and intention.
>
> • **Take to Go:** After infusing the charm with your
>   intention, carry it with you throughout the day.
>   Whenever you interact with it, take a moment
>   to reaffirm your intention and align your energy
>   with your desired outcome.

Lucky Girls Create Space for Luck to Flow In

Declutter your life, cut out the crap, and create some space.

This can be mental or physical – all that *stuff* is just weighing you down.

Luck can't come in when you're full to the brim.

Another law for your list, but one you're going to need to put in place ASAP to clear out any old junk to make space and a way for luck to flow in: **The Law of Subtraction.**

This law emphasises the importance of removing unnecessary clutter, distractions, and negative thoughts to improve your life. It suggests that by subtracting what is not mandatory from our lives, we can focus on what truly matters and increase our luck. Applying this law can help you manifest what you want by eliminating distractions and freeing up your mind for more fruitful actions.

This essential principle can apply to various fields, including science, mathematics, and business. The law entails removing or simplifying unnecessary elements to arrive at a more meaningful and efficient result, in doing so in any area of life, processes can become more streamlined, there's a reduction in waste, and you can achieve your goals more effectively.

The law of subtraction is closely related to the Pareto principle, or the 80/20 rule, which states that 80% of the effects come from 20% of the causes. This principle is relevant in business, where organisations can focus on the vital few rather than the trivial many, to maximise their efficiency and impact. For instance, companies can analyse their customer base and identify the most profitable clients to serve better while avoiding unprofitable or high-maintenance clients. Similarly, businesses can prioritise the products or services that generate the most revenue or value and cut back on those that do not contribute significantly.

The application of the law of subtraction is not limited to business but also extends to your Lucky Girl's personal development and well-being. According to research by psychologist Roy F. Baumeister, people have a limited amount of willpower and self-control, which they can exhaust by making too many decisions or tasks. By simplifying their choices and eliminating unnecessary decisions, they can conserve their willpower and make better choices in critical areas.[19] For instance, minimise your decision-making by automating routine tasks, establishing habits, or outsourcing irrelevant decisions to others.

Going back to school now for a lesson on Occam's Razor. This scientific method involves systematic and empirical investigation to test hypotheses and draw conclusions while avoiding unnecessary assumptions. Occam's Razor, named after a chap called William of Ockham, states that when multiple explanations exist for a phenomenon, the simplest explanation is usually the correct one. Therefore, even scientists and mathematicians use the law of subtraction to simplify problems, arrive at logical conclusions, and avoid overly complicated solutions.

The Law of Subtraction shows that decluttering and simplifying your life can lead to increased productivity, improved relationships, better physical health, and increased happiness. A study which explored the impact of home environments on well-being and stress found that individuals who live with clutter are more likely to experience stress, depression, and difficulty focusing on tasks compared to those who live in tidy environments. Moreover, the same study found that decluttering and organising improve mood and concentration, which can lead to better performance and increased luck.[20]

This law emphasises the importance of removing negative relationships and thoughts that can hold one back. Back to the incredible psychologist Carol Dweck (refer to Chapter 1), negative thoughts and beliefs can limit one's potential and decrease their ability to take risks, which is a critical component of manifesting what one wants. By subtracting negative thoughts and limiting beliefs, we open ourselves up to new opportunities, relationships, and experiences that can lead to increased luck.

Another way that the law of subtraction can help increase luck is by freeing up mental and physical space for more positive actions and habits. For example, removing negative relationships can open up time to develop new positive relationships, or clearing one's schedule can allow for time to pursue passions or hobbies. These positive actions can lead to increased luck and better opportunities that may not have been possible before.

In the realm of daily rituals, Marie Kondo, the renowned decluttering expert, offers a resonant example. Her practice of thanking objects before letting them go infuses the act of tidying up with mindfulness and gratitude. This ritual transforms decluttering from a chore into a purposeful act, aligning with her belief that a well-organized space enhances overall well-being.

Let the Law of Subtraction principle help conserve your resources, increase efficiency, allow you to arrive at logical conclusions, and reach your Lucky Girl Goals efficiently and effectively.

Subtract to attract.

The Debrief: The Unlucky Girl Detox

- **Identify:** Take a moment to identify areas of your life that are filled with negativity and clutter. This could include your physical environment, relationships, digital spaces, or even thought patterns. Write down the specific sources of negativity and clutter that you want to address.

- **Clean Up Mess:** Physical mess clogs up your mental environment. Choose one area, such as your bedroom, workspace, or a specific closet. Go through your belongings and decide what to keep, donate, or discard. Let go of items that no longer serve a purpose or bring you joy (akin to the Marie Kondo technique). As you declutter, visualise releasing not only physical clutter but also the negative energy associated with it.

- **Cleanse Your Digital Space:** Next, tackle your digital clutter. Organise your emails, files, and apps. Unfollow accounts on social media that promote negativity or make you feel drained. Create folders to categorise your digital content, making it easier to find what you need and reducing the mental clutter caused by disorganization.

- **Evaluate Your Relationships:** Reflect on your relationships and identify those that contribute to negativity . . . aka those energy vampires. This doesn't necessarily mean cutting people out of your life, but rather setting healthy boundaries for yourself and limiting your exposure to toxic dynamics. Create a list of people who raise your vibration, uplift you, and support and surround yourself with them. Great excuse to plan a date with them!

- **Shake Up Your Routine:** Create a positive ritual. Establish a daily ritual that promotes positivity and mental clarity. This could be mindfulness, meditation, yoga, or journaling. Engaging in these activities regularly can help you stay centred and resilient against negativity.

Nurture healthy habits and make choices that align with your well-being and happiness.

(*continued*)

(continued)

- **Lucky Girl Check-Ins:** Set aside time for regular check-ins to assess your progress. Revisit the areas you've decluttered and detoxed and celebrate the positive changes you've experienced. Take note of any lingering sources of negativity and adjust your approach accordingly. Go to gratitude or use your limiting beliefs tracker to consciously reframe and produce positivity. Don't let negative thought patterns clutter your mind.

Lucky Girls Surround Themselves with Lucky Souls and Share Their Lucky Girl Powers

Your vibe attracts your tribe / 'Birds of a feather flock together' / Lucky Girls gravitate towards Lucky Girls – however you see it, see it as truth.

Lucky Girls naturally gravitate towards one another, forming a community based on positivity, collaboration, and shared values. Actively engaged in building connections and networks, Lucky Girls leverage the power of community to expand their knowledge and access opportunities. This not only corroborates with the National Bureau of Economic Research's findings on the positive impact of social networks on job search outcomes but also underscores the scientific benefits of surrounding oneself with positive, like-minded individuals.

The advantages of such a community are numerous:

- **Increased Happiness:** Positive interactions with Lucky People contribute to elevated happiness levels, as the brain tends to mimic the emotions of those around us. The contagious nature of positivity can shape one's own attitude and outlook on life.

- **Stress Reduction:** Quality time with supportive individuals acts as a de-stressor, releasing endorphins and replacing cortisol levels with a sense of well-being. On the contrary, negative influences, often referred to as energy vampires, can exacerbate stress and should be minimised.

- **Improved Physical and Mental Health:** Research indicates that socially connected individuals make healthier lifestyle choices, fostering a sense of belonging, self-esteem, and confidence. Socialisation plays a crucial role in mental health, aiding individuals in coping with struggles and health difficulties.

- **Enhanced Resilience:** Lucky Girls, surrounded by a supportive community, develop positive coping strategies and resilience in the face of setbacks. Learning from the experiences of others and viewing failures as opportunities for growth become integral to this shared journey.

While challenging to remove negative influences entirely (hello, Energy Vampires!), the importance of actively seeking positive, like-minded individuals cannot be overstated. Whether through groups, clubs, or organizations aligned with personal values, connecting with Lucky People enriches life in ways science is only beginning to comprehend.

As a Lucky Girl, one becomes part of a network offering unwavering support. This community is a collective an open-minded, kind, and empathetic space where comfort and assistance are readily available. Engagement through social media, events, or email further enhances this network, emphasising that no Lucky Girl walks alone. More information is available on the website (https://lucky-collective.com/), where you can take the step to connect and thrive together. Join us and let's create some magic!

What's equally important is to share your Lucky Girl Powers!

Sharing Lucky Girl Syndrome is not just a choice; it's a commitment outlined in the Lucky Girl contract. The principle of 'like attracts like' encourages sharing knowledge and experiences to create a supportive and inspiring community where everyone can learn and grow together.

Despite potential challenges in finding like-minded individuals, the act of sharing Lucky Girl Syndrome can lead to personal and collective empowerment. By creating a sense of community, one gains support, encouragement, and motivation to stay committed to goals. Sharing success stories and personal experiences reinforces belief in the possibilities offered by Lucky Girl Syndrome and contributes to improved emotional well-being and life satisfaction.

Ultimately, sharing Lucky Girl Powers not only nurtures a positive mindset but also encourages collaboration and innovation. Embracing the collective power of manifestations allows Lucky Girls to combine expertise, perspectives, and approaches, discovering new techniques, applications, and possibilities in the shared journey toward luck and success.

Sharing also encourages collaboration and innovation. A study by Uzzi and Spiro found that diverse collaborative networks increase the likelihood of generating break-through ideas and creative solutions.[21] Facilitating an environment that embraces the collective power of manifestations allows you to combine your expertise, perspectives, and approaches to discovering new techniques, applications, and possibilities.

Get out there and share your Lucky Girl Powers with the world!

Lucky Girls See Well-Being as a Continuous Stream

If you don't schedule a break, your body will take one for you, and it probably won't be at a convenient time, which is why you should see well-being as a continuous stream, something that constantly needs to flow.

Well-being encompasses the harmony of body, mind, and spirit, allowing you to function optimally across various life domains, from work to emotional equilibrium, physical vitality, and mental clarity.

Lucky Girls are Well Girls!

Forget what you *THINK* is well-being and step away from preconceived notions of well-being that you may have seen on social media – the pretty, matching yoga sets, the crystal-infused water bottles, and the array of accessories straight out of the pages of GOOP (aka Gwyneth Paltrow's business empire). Wellness is the natural rhythm of existence, the very current of life.

Residing within the confines of limiting thoughts, dwelling on negativity, complaining, and harbouring resentment opposes the flow of life. In contrast, Lucky Girls effortlessly align themselves with the current of well-being, which makes attracting luck an inherent part of their lives.

Positive alignment characterises Lucky Girls, an alignment you too can forge by dismissing thoughts of scarcity, relinquishing resentment, and embracing the present as it is – recognising that life constantly propels you towards your well-being.

Nurturing your well-being stands paramount to a gratifying existence; it's integral to embodying the essence of a true Lucky Girl. Abandon the notion of transient well-being; envision it as an unbroken continuum that demands consistent dedication from you, Lucky Girl.

The World Health Organisation underscores mental well-being's dynamic nature, responsive to personal circumstances. Thus, well-being is a lifestyle, not an endpoint.

Embarking on your wellness voyage entails several steps.

Firstly, engage in regular physical activity, with studies showing its capacity to bolster physical and mental health while curbing chronic diseases. Exercise invigorates not just the body but also the mind, enhancing mood, memory, and mental clarity.

Next, prioritise mental health through practises like meditation, self-reflection, positive affirmations, or immersive hobbies. Such pursuits enhance emotional resilience, curb anxiety, and mitigate stress.

Nurturing relationships constitutes the third pillar, fortifying a network of support with loved ones, as outlined above. These connections offer solace during challenging times, affirming one's worth and providing a cushion of care.

When you board a plane, the pilot will say, 'In case of emergency, put on your own oxygen mask first before helping anyone else'. This is where self-care comes into play: see your oxygen mask as self-care, which saves your well-being, and in doing so, you can be better equipped to then help everyone else.

Treat yourself like you would a child – provide constant care and do things that make you feel good. Laugh.

Nourish your body with delicious and yummy foods. Hydrate. Treat yourself. Teach yourself. Be patient. Have naps. Have time-outs. Speak nicely to yourself. Be kind and compassionate. Hug yourself. Praise yourself. Surround yourself with love.

Lucky Girls are committed to self-nurturance because it bolsters alignment with well-being and attracts the desired currents of luck. After all, self-care isn't just an act; it's a way of saying to yourself that you are worth investing in. So, welcome self-care as a foundational building block of your Lucky Girl life, underpinning the continuous stream of well-being in your life.

The Debrief: Sacred Self-Care

Self-care is sacred. It's about honouring and nurturing yourself holistically. It's a beautiful way to develop self-love, mindfulness, and a deeper connection to your own inner wisdom. Make sacred self-care a regular part of your routine. **Schedule Time:** Block out time in your diary for self-care. Treat it as a non-negotiable appointment with yourself.

- **Identify Your Needs:** When it comes to your self-care date – pause and reflect on how you're feeling and what areas of your life need attention. Are you physically tired? Mentally stressed? Emotionally drained?

- **Pick Your Poison:** Choose one or two self-care activities that are manageable and realistic for your current schedule and energy level. In need of inspo for the self-care department? A great resource on the website (https://lucky-collective.com/) is a self-care cheat sheet, detailing cost-effective and easy-to-do self-care activities.

- **Rinse & Repeat:** After your self-care activity, reflect on how you feel. Did it provide relaxation, joy, or a sense of relief? Use this insight to adjust your self-care routine as needed and keep it going.

Lucky Girls Show Up Every Day

The most wonderful trait found in Lucky Girls is their unwavering ability to persevere through adversity. The capacity to show up each day, to confront whatever challenges we may face head-on, and to remain steadfast in pursuing goals becomes the gateway to increased resilience and expanded opportunities.

Even though there's no certainty about what tomorrow holds, and if indeed it will even come – the significance of being present today cannot be undermined. A study published in *Frontiers in Psychology*[22] highlights that individuals who view luck as a factor under their control, rather than beyond their influence tend to exhibit greater proactivity and tenacity in the pursuit of their objectives.

Our lives continually evolve, shaped by diverse experiences that shape our aspirations. Irrespective of these variables, it remains pivotal to approach each day with the intention of showing up as the best version of ourselves. Regardless of how you feel, this commitment is essential for multiple reasons: it sets the tone for your entire day and influences the way you approach challenges and opportunities. By making a conscious choice to show up with determination, you're not only cultivating a strong mindset but also sending a powerful message to the universe about your intentions. This consistent effort and positive energy are like magnets, drawing luck and favourable circumstances towards you.

Furthermore, this commitment has a profound impact on your personal growth. Every day presents a new chance to learn, improve, and evolve. By striving to be better, you're creating a positive feedback loop of growth and development. This process not only enhances your skills and capabilities but also builds your self-confidence and belief in your ability to overcome obstacles.

Progress is never linear, and there will be days when challenges seem insurmountable.

Maybe you had a shitty day, that's OK – there's tomorrow. And really, we can't even then guarantee that tomorrow will come!

However, the commitment to showing up and giving your best effort, and leading with love remains constant, even if you brace yourself for a shitty day ahead. If you can embrace the difficulties as opportunities for growth and resilience, you're taking a step closer to your Lucky Girl Goals and embodying the essence of creating your own luck.

Championing self-improvement by aiming to outdo our past selves every day becomes a habit. The practice of setting daily steps to tackle not only enhances feelings of accomplishment and productivity but also paves the way for achieving long-term objectives.[23] When you feel overwhelmed by your overarching Lucky Girl Goals, consider breaking them down into manageable steps. Incorporating that all-important question into your daily routine – like 'What's one small step I can take today towards my Lucky Girl Goal?' – can be instrumental.

This commitment to showing up radiates positivity and purpose, influencing those around us. The ripple effect of positivity ensues, inspiring others to follow suit. By embodying a positive outlook, you can create a transformative impact within your workplace, community, or even on a larger scale. This contributes to cultivating a more positive world.

Lucky Girl Syndrome aligns with those who persistently show up for themselves, even in the face of adversity. *'You don't attract what you want; you attract what you are'*, as Dr Wayne Dyer eloquently put it. Therefore, make a conscious effort to embody the finest version of yourself each day. Utilise those empowering Lucky Girl affirmations you've crafted, step out with confidence, and honour yourself with the commitment to continual growth and positivity.

To ensure that you present your best self not only tomorrow but in all your future endeavours, consider incorporating the following Lucky Girl Manifest Magic exercise into your daily routine. This exercise can significantly enhance your ability to manifest your deepest desires promptly and effectively, right in the present moment.

Performing this exercise before bedtime holds a special advantage: it sets a positive tone for the upcoming day, helping you wake up with a sense of purpose and determination. You'll find that as you engage in this practice consistently, your manifestation abilities grow stronger.

It's important to acknowledge that the power of our thoughts in shaping our reality is undeniable, and the influence of our words is even more immediate and potent. Through this exercise, you will delve deep into your subconscious mind, effectively reprogramming it to align with your desires.

With just three carefully chosen words, you will instantly harmonise your energy and frequency with your desires. This is a profound step towards ensuring that your manifestations are not just possibilities for the future but tangible realities in the making.

Right here, right now – I want you to **be sure.**

The Debrief: I'm Sure Method

- **Set the Intention:** Begin by closing your eyes and taking a moment to get very clear on what it is that you want to manifest. Think of your Lucky Girl Goals.

- **Affirmation:** Once you are clear on your intention, affirm it out loud using the phrase 'I'm Sure'. State your intention in the present tense, as if it has already happened. For example:

  'I'm sure I got the promotion.'

  'I'm sure X texted me back.'

  'I'm sure I make £100,000.'

- **Repeat 10 Times:** Repeat this affirmation out loud 10 times. As you do so, try to feel the emotions associated with your desire as if it's already a reality. Imagine the joy, satisfaction, and gratitude that come with achieving your goal.

- **Bonus – Write it Down:** For added reinforcement, write down your affirmation on a piece of paper. This can help solidify your intention and commitment to manifesting your desire.

(continued)

(*continued*)

- **Continuous Repetition:** Throughout the day, whenever your desire pops into your mind or you find yourself doubting it, repeat the affirmation to yourself, 'I am sure . . .'. This helps keep your focus on your intention and reinforces your belief in its realisation.

7

One Golden Rule

'I'll be happy when xyz happens'; 'I'll feel settled when I make £££'; 'I'll be successful when I xyz'; 'I'll be able to love myself when I meet the perfect partner'; or 'I'll finally be happy when dreams come true'.

I'm so sorry to tell you – 'when' is probably not coming, and it likely never will.

Now, I'm very guilty of this.

If I had to pinpoint the exact moment my 'whens' started, it was probably back in school during the pre-pubescent glory days. All the girls in my year were suddenly coming into school as women – boobs popping up literally overnight, and growing so tall they would make me look like Frodo Baggins, and conversations were all about snogging boys and going to first base. Little, naive me, on the other hand, hadn't been kissed let alone approached by a boy, would stuff my bra, and hadn't even experienced my first period. I was what you call a 'late bloomer'. Because of how I looked compared to my peers, I would be teased and mocked. One time, after an awful encounter with the school big-boobed bully, who cornered me in the changing rooms after a sports class and pinched my nipples to try to 'bring my tits out', I was so traumatised that I asked my mum to look into transferring schools.

I would desperately think to myself *I'll be happy when I get my period because then my boobs will come in, I'll look like the other girls, and the teasing will stop.* The bully moved on to the next victim, I didn't change schools and cracked back on life the way a 14-year-old would. Fast forward a few months, and as an early Christmas present, my period came.

Was I finally happy? *Absolutely not.* I was horrified, in pain as I'd never experienced before, confused, grumpy, and hated anyone in plain sight.

Ironically, it was the worst gift I have ever received.

Following 'periodgate', my *when* quickly changed to *I'll be happy when I leave school*, fantasising about the day I'd be free and independent, with a fresh new start at college. Then it would be *I'll be happy when I can drive, I'll be happy when he notices me, I'll be happy when I go to university* – you get the picture.

Even when grown up in my 20s and becoming more self-aware, I'd often still find 'when' creeping back in – *I'll be happy when I look like her, I'll definitely know if I'm good at my job when I get that promotion, I'll be happy when he changes, I'll be happy when I meet someone else, I'll be happy when he takes it to the next stage* . . . you get the picture.

The line just keeps on moving, doesn't it?

We get what we want, then realise it didn't solve all of our life issues and insecurities, so we look outward again and choose the next *'I'll be happy when'.*

We don't actually have a lot of control over how or what happens to us from an external perspective, but the problem is when we fixate on the internal milestones of 'when' it sabotages the joy we find in our lives in the now.

In other words: in our pursuit of happiness, we end up postponing present joy.

It's sad to reflect on all the numerous times we've been too focused on our 'whens', but it's even sadder to carry on being unaware. This pursuit of 'when' – searching to meet desires, experiences, and aspirations – is a natural and intrinsic part of life. We set our Lucky Girl Goals, work hard, and strive to achieve what we want, believing that it will bring us happiness and fulfilment. However, it is not uncommon to experience a sense of emptiness or dissatisfaction even after attaining our long-desired goals or getting to that place we've dreamt about going and feeling disappointed. Understanding the Lucky Girl Golden Rule, which we will come on to shortly, we understand the complexities of desire fulfilment and the illusion of resolution so we can approach the manifestation process with greater awareness and find true contentment.

We *Think* We Know What We Want

Being exposed to a world where success is often seen on a very shallow level. What luxury possessions we have, how much money is in our accounts, what the title of our role is, what car we drive, etc., isn't wrong, but it sure is messing with you because – guess what? – there's *always* going to be someone richer, thinner, and taller than you, with more Instagram followers, better hair, and bigger boobs BUT there is only, and will ever only, be **one of you**. And how amazing is that?

The best piece of advice I've ever heard is this:

If it doesn't bring you energy, inspiration, or an orgasm, then you don't need it.

I mean, wow. How true are these words?

Having experience in both the social media and wellness sectors, I've witnessed the harmful impact of the *'I'll be happy when'* mentality. Working with high-profile individuals, successful entrepreneurs, and seemingly content people, I've noticed how they, too, fall into the trap of chasing their next *'I'll be happy when'* goal.

This mindset leads us to believe that we must alter our bodies or possess certain material possessions to find happiness. We strive to fix parts of ourselves that were beautiful all along, and we feel pressured to attain specific cars, clothes, or other possessions and have a certain figure in our bank account, assuming it will bring us joy. And guess what? It doesn't make you any happier!

The truth is that these external achievements or changes do not guarantee lasting happiness. They might momentarily satisfy us, but the fulfilment we seek cannot be found solely in external circumstances. It lies within us, in our ability to appreciate and embrace who we are and what we have in the present moment. True happiness comes from cultivating a positive mindset and finding contentment with ourselves as we are.

Getting to grips with this is a huge step in knowing you're well on your way in the process of healing, growth, and luck.

The Illusion of Fulfilment

The moment we attain what we want, there is an initial rush of joy and excitement. We bask in the accomplishment and anticipate a sense of resolution to our problems and insecurities. However, this euphoria is usually short-lived. Psychologists refer to this as the 'hedonic treadmill' phenomenon, where we quickly adapt to positive changes in our lives, leading to a return to our baseline level of happiness. This adaptation suggests that external achievements have a limited long-term impact on our overall well-being.[1]

Moreover, the satisfaction derived from external accomplishments tends to be conditional and fleeting. When we solely rely on external validation or material possessions to feel complete, we overlook the deeper aspects of our well-being that contribute to lasting fulfilment.

A classic case study on the illusion involves lottery winners. Brickman et. al. found that despite their significant financial windfall, lottery winners were no happier than individuals who did not win the lottery.[2] In fact, many of the winners reported a decline in overall life satisfaction after an initial period of elation. This case study highlights how external achievements may not provide lasting happiness or resolve underlying issues and insecurities.

The Cycle of Seeking More

The cycle of seeking more after fulfilling your desire can be attributed to several psychological factors. Social comparison plays a role in driving individuals to compare themselves with others who have achieved more or possess something desirable. This comparison can lead to feelings of inadequacy or a fear of missing out, prompting individuals to continuously strive for more.

The pursuit of desires is often fuelled by the belief that achieving the next goal will finally provide lasting contentment. This pursuit, known as the 'arrival fallacy', implies that happiness is a destination, attainable only when specific goals are met.[3] However, such beliefs can create a never-ending quest for external validation, leaving individuals perpetually unsatisfied.

Successful entrepreneurs may have achieved financial success but still grapple with feelings of emptiness and dissatisfaction. Celebrities with fame and adoration may struggle with mental health challenges despite external adulation. Material accomplishments do not guarantee inner peace or the resolution of deeper insecurities.

Arianna Huffington, the co-founder of The Huffington Post, went through exactly this.

Since founding The Huffington Post in 2005, it has become one of the most popular news websites globally. Under her leadership, The Huffington Post grew into a major media outlet and won numerous awards for its journalism.

Arianna became a figure of entrepreneurial success and gained global recognition.

In 2007, she collapsed from exhaustion and burnout, attributing the incident to her relentless pursuit of success at the expense of her health and personal life. This was the wake-up call that led her to re-evaluate her life and focus on her well-being, detailing that the experience made her realise that the traditional markers of success – wealth, fame, and power – were not enough to bring true happiness.

In the aftermath of her burnout, Huffington became an advocate for well-being and redefined success to include aspects beyond financial achievements. She authored several books on the subject, including *Thrive: The Third Metric to Redefining Success and Creating a Life of Well-Being, Wisdom, and Wonder,*[4] where she champions the importance of well-being, sleep, and mindfulness in achieving a balanced and fulfilling life. Huffington's story highlights the common struggle among successful entrepreneurs, regardless of gender, to find genuine contentment and purpose beyond financial success and underscores the need for a more holistic definition of success that includes personal growth, happiness, and overall well-being.

Well-being and life satisfaction are not solely dependent on financial success but are influenced by factors such as social connections, work–life balance, and a sense of purpose.[5] Achieving financial success is undoubtedly an important goal, but it should not be the sole focus. Successful female entrepreneurs, like Arianna Huffington, demonstrate the significance of supporting a broader perspective on success, one that integrates personal growth, emotional well-being, and meaningful connections into the journey of entrepreneurship.

Beyond a Lucky Life

In a world where the *'I'll be happy when'* mentality prevails, it is vital to shift our focus towards acceptance of the present moment. Instead of continuously seeking external validation or material achievements, we must cherish what truly matters.

Without sounding too morbid, at some point, we will all die and leave whatever luck we've generated in our lives behind.

In whatever form and whatever your belief, when we leave this world, we take absolutely nothing with us. The house we call home, our possessions, our loved ones, our pets, etc. all stay here on earth.

Physically, these things do not accompany us beyond death.

Sure, we live on through stories and memories, but really, the things we accumulate over the span of our lifetime have no significance beyond our time here. In the face of mortality, this notion facilitates our focus on the intangible aspects of life and the legacy we leave.

Reading this, be encouraged when setting our Lucky Girl Goals to shift your perspective from the pursuit of materials, wealth, and external validations and instead place greater importance on meaningful connections, relationships, personal growth, and the impact we have on others.

Take a moment to contemplate your values, beliefs, and the impression you want to leave behind. Align your actions with your core values and prioritise the present moment. Embrace experiences and adventures over the accumulation of possessions. Invest in your relationships, for they bring joy, love, and fulfilment.

Nurture this mindset of focusing on what truly matters to you. This is how you leave a positive legacy that extends beyond your time on Earth, impacting others in a meaningful way. Cherish each moment and let the essence of your life be defined by the relationships you nurture and the experiences you create.

The Avoidance of Now

In our daily lives, we often engage in activities that inadvertently pull us away from the present moment, preventing us from fully experiencing life's richness. These seemingly normal pastimes can lead to an escape from the present rather than enriching our lives.

For instance, drinking alcohol, scrolling on social media, shopping, gambling, etc. are all socially acceptable ways to pass the time. However, when these activities are used as a way of avoidance, e.g., drinking alcohol to numb pain, scrolling on social media to escape, compulsively shopping, taking recreational drugs, or gambling, they can take their toll and become harmful to our well-being.

Various scientific disciplines have studied and explored the psychological phenomenon of avoidance. Here are some explanations from several psychological theories:

- **Evolutionary Psychology:** One perspective suggests that our tendency to avoid the present moment may have evolved as a survival mechanism. From the very beginning, when humans first walked on earth, being vigilant about potential threats and dangers in the environment was crucial for survival. This 'fight or flight' response kept our ancestors alert and prepared to react to potential dangers. In modern times, this evolutionary response can translate into constant vigilance, anxiety, and difficulty being present, as our brains are wired to scan for potential problems and challenges.

- **Cognitive Bias:** Cognitive biases are systematic errors in thinking that influence our perceptions and judgements. A 'negativity bias' is where we tend to give more weight to negative experiences and emotions than positive ones. This bias allows you to ruminate on past negative events or worry about future challenges, making it challenging to fully engage with the present moment.

- **Psychological Time Travel:** We possess the unique ability to mentally travel through time, imagining the past and the future. While this capacity has many advantages, such as planning and learning from past experiences, it can also lead to a preoccupation with past regrets or future anxieties. The concept of 'psychological time travel' suggests that our minds are constantly shifting between past, present, and future, making it difficult to fully inhabit the present moment.

- **Avoidance Coping:** Avoidance coping is a psychological strategy where we avoid facing or dealing with challenging emotions, situations, or stressors. When faced with uncomfortable feelings or difficult tasks, sometimes we may choose distractions or engage in activities that take our minds away from the present. While this coping mechanism may provide temporary relief, it can lead to a cycle of avoidance and hinder emotional growth and resilience.

· **Attachment Styles:** Those with insecure attachment styles, such as anxious or avoidant attachment, may struggle with being present in relationships and have difficulty forming secure connections. These attachment patterns can manifest in adulthood as difficulty staying present in social interactions and experiencing intimacy.

Understanding the psychological underpinnings of why we avoid the present moment helps you develop strategies to develop mindfulness and embrace the richness of life in the here and now.

Without further ado, to comb it back into the now follow the golden rule of:

A present, accepting attitude and profound gratitude creates Lucky Girl magnitude.

In each and every moment, you make choices that affect your present and future. So, why not learn how to use the present moment to attract more of what you want?

Acceptance is a transformative power. It's the cornerstone of inner peace and the foundation upon which personal growth is built. Accepting life, who you are, how you feel, your circumstances, etc. does not mean resignation; it means acknowledging the reality of the present moment. It allows you to work from where you are, with what you have. By accepting who you are, with all your strengths and flaws, you liberate yourself from the burden of self-criticism and open the door to self-love.

Acceptance is a profound form of self-compassion.

When you accept your circumstances, your identity, your emotions, and the ebb and flow of life, you free yourself from unnecessary suffering. You live in the present, unburdened by the weight of what should have been or what might be. This acceptance is not a passive surrender but an active, courageous choice to engage with life as it is.

In this acceptance, you find the strength to change what you can, the courage to endure what you can't, and the wisdom to know the difference. It's a profound act of self-love and a gateway to a life lived with authenticity, resilience, and a deep sense of peace.

The human experience encompasses both joy and suffering, and how we respond to challenging situations significantly impacts our lives and our ability to create our own luck.

Non-acceptance of our present moment, often driven by resistance to reality, can perpetuate suffering and hinder our ability to find peace.

'I'll be happy when' is essentially a non-acceptance of the present moment.

This refers to the resistance and aversion to the current reality, which can manifest in various ways, such as denial, avoidance, or frustration. It is a common human tendency and totally understandable to want things to be different than they are and change the now, especially during challenging or distressing situations. However, this resistance to our current situation can intensify suffering, prolong emotional pain, and reign of bad luck.

In the fields of psychology and mindfulness, an exploration into the relationship between non-acceptance and suffering has shown those who struggle with accepting distressing emotions or difficult life circumstances are more likely to experience heightened levels of anxiety, depression, and overall psychological distress.[6]

A study conducted by Kashdan and Breen found participants who exhibited non-acceptance tendencies reported greater difficulties in managing negative emotions, leading to increased distress and lower overall life satisfaction.[7]

Acceptance and Commitment Therapy (ACT) suggests that the presence of suffering often indicates a lack of acceptance. In this therapeutic approach, pain is recognised as a natural part of life, even though it is undesirable. Emotional distress is considered a valid and appropriate response to challenging life events. However, suffering arises when we experience pain and simultaneously resist or refuse to accept it.

This resistance to acceptance can take various forms, such as:

- Holding those rigid rules along with beliefs about how things 'should' or 'shouldn't' be.

  'I should be luckier and further along by now' or 'I shouldn't be experiencing such bad luck'.

- Engaging in unproductive questioning, seeking answers that are unavailable or unhelpful.

  'Why did this happen? If only things were different)... What if...?'

  'If only I was more like abc, then I could succeed at xyz'.

- Being unwilling to accept the reality of what has already occurred or the current circumstances.

  'Why does bad luck always happen to me?'

When we struggle against the present reality, suffering arises. The goal is to cultivate acceptance of our experiences, including pain and discomfort, while committing to actions that align with our values and move us towards a more meaningful and vital life. By practising acceptance, we can reduce unnecessary suffering, find greater peace in the face of life's challenges, and create lasting luck.

'Two countries at war' is a metaphor used by psychologist Russ Harris to illustrate the difference between acceptance and resignation/tolerance.[8]

In this metaphor, he compares two imaginary countries:

- **The Land of Acceptance:** In this country, the inhabitants acknowledge and face their challenges and difficulties head-on. They recognise the reality of their circumstances and emotions without judgement or resistance. They don't deny the existence of problems, but they don't get caught up in fighting against them either. Instead, they embrace the struggles as a natural part of life and focus on taking effective action to improve their situation.

- **The Land of Resignation/Tolerance:** This country's inhabitants, on the other hand, have a different approach. They also face difficulties, but they do so with a sense of resignation or tolerance. They may be aware of their problems, but they don't believe they have the power to change anything. As a result, they endure their struggles without actively seeking solutions, feeling helpless and stuck in their circumstances.

The fundamental difference between the two countries lies in how their inhabitants respond to challenges:

- **The Land of Acceptance:** This emphasises mindfulness, where individuals stay present with their experiences and emotions, even if they are uncomfortable. They recognise that negative emotions are a normal part of life and choose not to let those emotions dictate their actions or well-being.

- **The Land of Resignation/Tolerance:** Promotes avoidance and denial. The inhabitants are more likely to suppress their emotions or try to distract themselves from their difficulties. They may believe that accepting their circumstances means giving up, and as a result, they don't take any constructive steps to improve their situation.

Harris uses this metaphor to encourage people to adopt a more mindful and accepting approach to life's challenges. He suggests that acceptance is not about being passive or tolerating misery; rather, it is about acknowledging reality and choosing to respond to difficulties in a way that aligns with one's values and goals. Acceptance empowers individuals to make positive changes and take effective action, even amidst difficult circumstances.

In summary, the metaphor of 'two countries at war' illustrates the difference between acceptance and resignation/tolerance and emphasises the importance of tackling challenges with mindfulness and peaceful, proactive problem-solving.

How to Now

Utilise the power of the present moment to enhance your manifestations, Lucky Girl. It is in the here and now that you hold the key to creating and attracting new, thrilling experiences. Utilise the present as your canvas for bringing your desires to life and inviting positive changes into your Lucky Girl Life, and here's how . . .

Mindful Manifesting

Imagine yourself as living in The Land of Acceptance. To become a model-like citizen of this land, and thrive, drawing desires to you, you're going to have to get on board with the country's policies – whereby you acknowledge the truth of your situation without denial or evasion, yet refrain from getting entangled in a constant struggle against challenges. You can easily do this through mindfulness practice.

Mindfulness, a practice of being fully present and non-judgemental, plays a crucial role in promoting acceptance. By practising mindfulness, you develop a greater awareness of your thoughts and emotions without clinging to or resisting them. Mindfulness-based interventions have been found to reduce symptoms of anxiety, depression, and stress by encouraging participants to accept their experiences and feelings without judgement.[9]

When speaking about mindfulness, it never fails to surprise me to hear how hard people find it. Everyone agrees they know it's a good, if not, great, thing to do, but then gets put off.

We have in our heads what we *think* mindfulness is or looks like. I used to despise anything related to meditation and mindfulness because I used to think that way too. I had this fixed idea that it required sitting cross-legged like a Buddhist monk or yogi, for a longggg amount of time, trying to clear my mind completely of all thoughts until I reached enlightenment.

With this misconception, I found it incredibly challenging. Moreover, as someone with ADHD, sitting still has always been a struggle. It would bring back memories of my pre-school days, where I'd get reprimanded for not sitting quietly with my legs crossed and for fidgeting. These memories often disrupted my mindfulness practice, leading to a flood of random thoughts, then I'd find myself fidgeting more and getting even more lost in my head, and in the time I set aside to meditate, it would make me more anxious than I was to begin with! The exact opposite of what mindfulness aims to achieve.

Coming to the realisation that mindfulness is simply about acceptance of the moment, your relationship with it will drastically change. It's not about forcing anything, but just being present and acknowledging the moment for what it is, without judgement or resistance. It's about letting go and allowing the experience to unfold naturally. Meditation or mindfulness doesn't have to look any particular way; you can do it tucked up in bed, lying down, or cosying up in a chair. You can do it for three minutes or thirty. You don't necessarily need to surround yourself with candles and incense (although it does create a lovely, calming atmosphere), you don't have to set up a shrine; and you certainly don't need to put yourself under pressure thinking you'll reach enlightenment in 10 minutes. This newfound understanding has transformed my approach to mindfulness, making it a more rewarding and fulfilling practice, and if you too have a love/hate relationship with it, please be encouraged to define your own version of what mindfulness looks like to you and try to stick at it.

Allow mindfulness to help you appreciate and cherish the present moment.

On the website (https://lucky-collective.com/), you will find guided mindful meditation practices to help you draw yourself back to now.

Breathe

The breath is one of the most powerful tools our bodies harness.

If you're living, you're breathing. So if you are living and breathing, you can use your breath to help you come back to the present moment – no excuses!

Facilitating nicely with mindfulness, meditation, and yoga, the breath acts as an anchor to settle you into now by engaging the body's relaxation response, improving attention and focus, enhancing emotional regulation, and creating positive changes in the brain.

The advantages of using our breath are these:

- **Physiological Effects:** Deep breathing activates the body's parasympathetic nervous system, which is responsible for the 'rest and digest' response. This activation leads to a reduction in the production of stress hormones like cortisol and adrenaline, promoting a sense of relaxation and calmness.

- **Attention and Focus:** As we breathe mindfully, we direct our awareness to the sensation of each inhale and exhale. Intentional focus helps train the mind to stay present, as it continually brings attention back to the breath whenever thoughts or distractions arise.

- **Emotional Regulation:** Breath-focused practices can positively impact emotional regulation and increases our ability to respond more skilfully. By creating space between stimulus and response, you gain a greater understanding of emotions without becoming overwhelmed by them.

- **Neural Correlates:** Neuroimaging studies have shown that breath-focused techniques can lead to changes in brain activity and structure. Regular practice has been associated with increased grey matter density in brain regions linked to attention, emotion regulation, and self-awareness.

The Debrief: Box Breath

Following this four-step pattern, you create a calming and balanced rhythm, similar to the shape of the square.

Place your book down and give it a go:

- Inhale slowly and deeply through your nose for a count of four.

- Hold your breath for a count of four.

- Exhale slowly and completely through your mouth for a count of four.

- Pause and hold your breath for another count of four.

Repeat this cycle for several rounds, focusing on the rhythmic pattern of breathing.

Now, check back in with yourself – how do you feel?

EFT / Tapping

Want to slow down and quiet down the mental chatter?

EFT is your BFF.

The basics have been covered for luck (see Chapter 6), but did you know it's energetically one of the best ways to help you let go of the past, release the future, and bring you back into the present?

EFT tapping (Emotional Freedom Technique) complements mindfulness by tapping on specific meridian points, encouraging you to acknowledge and verbalise your current emotions, thoughts, and experiences. This process helps to shift the focus away from ruminative thinking and redirect attention to the physical act of tapping and the present sensations in the body.

As a result, you are able to observe your emotions from a more detached perspective, which aids in self-compassion and self-awareness.

Through rounds of tapping, you are actively releasing negative energy, reducing emotional reactivity, and providing a direct connection to yourself. This somatic awareness promotes a deeper sense of self and allows you to respond to challenges in a more balanced and constructive manner, adding to the Lucky Girl resilience you're already creating.

On the website (https://lucky-collective.com/) you'll find a tapping script and guided meditation to bring you back into the now.

Gratitude

Incorporating the magnificent mystical powers of gratitude into the present moment can significantly enhance you and your outlook on life.

Gratitude is like a magnifying glass for positivity in your life. When you cultivate gratitude, you shift your focus from what you lack to what you have, helping you see the good in your life, no matter how small. When Lucky Girls harness the potent force of gratitude and apply it to their present moments, they unlock a gateway to appreciating the beauty in the ordinary, making stronger connections, and experiencing a heightened awareness of their surroundings.

Don't overcomplicate it. Practising gratitude amidst a challenging present moment entails recognising and valuing even the tiniest positive aspects of your situation, which doesn't negate the difficulties but rather allows a balanced perspective. It's a conscious effort to shift your focus from the hardships to the moments of support, growth, and relief. This approach cultivates emotional resilience, providing a beacon of hope and positivity during tough times.

When we are in the present, and that state taps into gratitude, you can bet that you are attracting the things you want into your life because you are guided toward a more centred approach, uncovering hidden blessings and encouraged to see beyond immediate struggles.

The present moment is all we have. Make peace with it.

Quieting the inner turmoil allows us to check in with ourselves and fully engage with the present moment. Let go of resistance and accept the here and now with openness and gratitude, finding peace in the present.

Seeking out professional help or therapy can be immensely beneficial in making peace with your current circumstances and provide a safe and supportive environment to explore your emotions, thoughts, and challenges. Therapy can be a transformative process that helps develop a deeper understanding of yourself, your circumstances, and how to move forward with resilience and a sense of inner peace. Reaching out for help is a sign of strength and self-care, and it can lead to profound positive changes in your life.

Romanticise

This ain't delulu – romanticise your life, Lucky Girl!

It's going to help you appreciate and see all the beauty that comes with living in the present moment. By romanticising your life, you can cultivate a sense of wonder and enchantment, allowing you to find joy in the simplest of things. Embracing this mindset can also deepen your connections with others and create lasting memories that will make your life truly extraordinary.

I adore using this tool of romanticising my life, especially when after a low period. Through the art of romanticising, I've learned that life is not merely to be lived; it is to be cherished, savoured, and celebrated in all its breathtaking splendour. Every conversation becomes a chance to explore the unique universe within another person, discovering constellations of thoughts and emotions previously uncharted. Laughter becomes a melody, reminding me of the infectious nature of happiness. Even in the silent pauses between words, there exists a language of the soul, a silent understanding that transcends the boundaries of speech. When you live in the present and that perspective of the present is shifted in this way, you become both the audience and the protagonist, marvelling at the intricate plot twists and also able to feel more secure in life's emotional crescendos.

Steps to Romanticise

1. **Find art in the mundane:** Can you be open to seeing the beauty in your everyday, 'normal' tasks? If it's raining outside on a gloomy day, focus on the aroma of rain-kissed earth. On your boring commute to work, feel the warmth of a shared smile with a stranger. See that with every sunrise, you are reborn, embracing the day with open arms, ready to explore the endless possibilities that lie ahead. In the gentle caress of the wind, the soft touch of a loved one, and the taste of a homemade meal, find the poetry of life written in the simplest gestures. These celebrations of fleeting moments are a recognition that even the most ephemeral experiences possess a kind of magic that can leave an indelible mark on your heart.

2. **Surround yourself with inspiration:** Fill your surroundings with things that inspire you, whether it's artwork, music, or books. Creating an environment that sparks your imagination can ignite a sense of romance and creativity in your everyday life.

    Creativity is a gateway to the soul, allowing you to express your emotions and ideas in a tangible way.

3. **Slow down:** Flow slowly through life. Notice more in the world around you. Stop rushing and calm that busy, beautiful mind of yours.

4. **Nurture meaningful connections:** Seek out deep and meaningful relationships with others, whether it's through engaging conversations, heartfelt gestures, or acts of kindness. Nurturing these connections can bring a sense of romance. Genuine connections add depth and deeper meaning to your experience here on earth.

5. **Engage in romantic activities:** Engage in activities that encourage mindfulness, presence, and of course, romance. Take long walks in nature, throw a party for no good reason, wear that outfit that makes you feel fabulous, do something spontaneous, or cook a fancy meal with loved ones. Don't overcomplicate it – simply can infuse your life with sparks of joy and an abundance of appreciation.

By incorporating these practices into your daily life, you not only romanticise your existence but also create a profound shift in your perspective.

Through this lens, life is not just a series of events but a grand adventure, an epic tale waiting to be told. It transforms ordinary moments into extraordinary memories, making every day a chapter in a storybook of wonder and enchantment.

Don't Save the Good Candles

When it comes to 'whens' we tend to get caught up in the pursuit of future happiness and success, neglecting the beauty of the present moment. In this relentless pursuit, often we find ourselves saving our best experiences, possessions, and moments for a time we deem more fitting.

Ultimately, we don't know what tomorrow will bring. Life is short and unpredictable, and we should not take it for granted. Everything in life, including life itself, has an expiration date. Postponing our happiness, saving things for a better time, and waiting for these 'perfect moments', we risk missing out on the fulfilment that can be found in the present, and may even miss our own sell-by dates!

I'm very guilty of this – I used to constantly put off things that brought me joy because I'd opt to wait for the 'right' time instead. I've hoarded numerous items over the years, waiting to use them for certain events. Never used certain teacups in case the King of England would pop round. Saved my 'posh' candles. Kept outfits for good occasions. Left shoes in boxes unworn. Passed up job offers. Declined invitations for travel, thinking I'll wait until I have more time or more money. I've postponed enrolling in certain classes, believing I need to wait until my skills improve on my own. I've delayed reconnecting with old friends, assuming I'll reach out when I have something substantial to share. Or not connected with new, in fears they will judge me.

All these instances share a common thread: a tendency to delay joy and opportunities, under the illusion that a more suitable moment will present itself. It's akin to putting off the opening of a beautifully wrapped gift, waiting for a grand occasion that may never arrive.

A most recent example – for years and years, I saved a very special bottle of champagne to be popped opened at a very 'special' occasion. There were the key birthdays of my 18th, 21st, 30th (and all the ones in between), job promotions, buying my first house, there was my engagement and I would still find an excuse not to open and wait for *the* moment. Finally for my wedding, I couldn't think of a better moment – can you imagine the sheer disappointment finding out that 'special' bottle, because it had been left too long and stored incorrectly – was now corked?!

I've come to realise that there is no better time than now to embrace the things that make us happy and live life to the fullest. Understanding the fallacy of waiting for the 'right' time has inspired a shift in my approach. I've started to act spontaneously, finding charm in impromptu adventures. I've begun classes, embracing the process of learning without worrying about perfection. I've reached out to old friends and made new, appreciating the value of genuine connections, irrespective of the time passed. It's help me become more connected with myself and the universe around me and stop taking life for granted.

By seizing the present moment, we can create a life filled with cherished memories and meaningful experiences, rather than regretting what we didn't do when we had the chance. If, as reading this, you see yourself doing the same, reflecting on these missed opportunities is not a cause for regret, but rather an opportunity for growth and change. It's never too late to start appreciating the present, to relish the small moments, and to create your own perfect occasion.

It's time to break free from the cycle of postponement and start living by the philosophy: 'Don't save the good candles'.

The 'don't save the good candles' theory is a metaphor for not delaying joy or happiness for the future. Instead of keeping the good candles stashed away for a special event that might never come, light them up today.

At its core, 'don't save the good candles' signifies understanding that life's special occasions are not limited to grand celebrations; they encompass the entirety of our existence. It urges us to light up the metaphorical candles – symbolic of our happiness, passion, and dreams – right now, rather than waiting for a distant tomorrow.

This philosophy is not just a call to action; it's a transformative way of living, grounded in mindfulness, gratitude, and the science of well-being. In essence, this theory promotes the idea of living in the now and is a reminder that life is made up of a series of moments, and each moment is an opportunity to cherish and relish.

Here are some examples of how Lucky Ones can apply the 'don't save the good candles' theory to their lives:

- A Lucky Girl might choose to wear their favourite outfit to work instead of saving it for a special occasion.

- A Lucky Couple might choose to go out on a date night every week instead of waiting for a special anniversary or holiday.

- A Lucky Family might choose to travel to a new place every year instead of waiting until their children are older.

- A Lucky Girl might choose to start their own business instead of waiting until they have a lot of money saved up.

Work with this theory alongside romanticising your life – practising the 'don't save the good candles' philosophy is a deliberate choice, a commitment to finding joy in the ordinary. This mindset encourages us to transform routine activities into moments of significance and imbue our lives with a sense of celebration. Like with 'whens', those perfect moments may never come, so don't wait for it; make the moment perfect by living in the now.

Gently remind yourself daily – don't save those damn candles!

Your Purpose = Presence

All you can ever hope for in life is that you live your days in a way that's authentic, true, and meaningful to you.

We all possess an innate desire and intrinsic need for purpose in our life. It provides a sense of direction and reason for existence. Life events, challenges, trauma, loss, or major significant life transition moments prompt us to question what we are put on earth for and find deeper meaning in these experiences.

As society places a strong emphasis an achievement, success, and making a significant impact, often we feel societal pressure to have a clear purpose that aligns with these standards, leading to the intense need of finding what the hell it is.

That belief that a clear life purpose will ensure our fulfilment, happiness, and a sense of accomplishment, associating purpose with a better quality of life is what drives us.

We get far too caught up in 'finding our life's purpose', and it becomes a relentless diversion, trying to seek it out. Being future-oriented has become synonymous with the idea of purpose . . . and it isn't the only way you can feel purposeful.

We get told to *'follow your passion'*, *'find your purpose'*, *and 'figure out the meaning of life'* when at times we are struggling. And whilst finding our purpose in life is an enriching experience, maybe it doesn't have to be so complicated.

Maybe your life's purpose could be, *just to be.*

Struggling to know what your life purpose is? Then look no further:

Your purpose is to be solely present in each given moment and fully live in the now.

Like purpose, maybe your success too doesn't have to look a certain way. Only you can define your own level of success, so maybe stop overcomplicating this as well!

Success = being accepting of the present and fully open to whatever the moment brings.

No matter what form the present moment shapes, stop opposing it in your mind and just allow for it to be the way it is.

This may seem counterintuitive to your beautiful brain to accept a reality that gives you every reason to perceive it as 'bad', but if you accept it the way it is, it opens the gateway to bring in new solutions and good luck into your existence.

There really is only now and it's up to you Lucky Girl to live authentically in the present moment and truly be grateful for it. It's where our experiences unfold, and where we have the power to make choices and take action. Seeing our purpose as whatever the present is allows us to fully engage with life's beauty and challenges, making the most of every opportunity – all necessary qualities for living a Lucky Girl Life. The present moment affirms that life is ever-changing, and nothing remains the same. Embracing impermanence helps us let go of attachments and accept the transient nature of life, promoting a sense of peace and acceptance.

Eckhart Tolle beautifully sums it up: 'Realize deeply that the present moment is all you have. Make the NOW the primary focus of your life.'[10]

Making present-moment awareness of your life's purpose opens the door to a more mindful, intentional, and gratifying life. By choosing to live in the now, we can savour the richness of life, acquire deeper connections, and embrace the beauty of impermanence. It is an endless process of self-discovery and growth that leads to a life filled with purpose, joy, and contentment.

You are so nearly there, Lucky Girl – **accept what is.**

'When' may never come and, I hate to tell you, it probably never will. There is only now. It's not about being happy and positive all the time – it's about accepting the present for what it is and working with our emotions.

You may be seriously stuck in life right now. It may be pretty f*cking awful, and right now you may feel that you cannot face tomorrow, but my darlings, be gentle, as this too shall pass.

Accept life. Accept your circumstances. Accept who you are. Accept how you feel.

Accepting that your best days might still be ahead and that your worst days are temporary. Accept the impermanence of life. Life is a series of peaks and valleys, and in accepting this rhythm, you learn to savour the good moments and endure the difficult ones with Lucky Girl Grace.

Stop. Breathe. Re-Focus.

The Debrief: Coming Back to Now

Each time you feel overwhelmed, struggling, or pulled away from the present, try the following sequence:

- **Notice and label:** This is all about defusing your current experience, creating distance, and gaining perspective.

  Example: 'I'm feeling frustrated right now', 'I'm so upset', or 'I'm so pissed off'.

- Ask yourself, 'What am I not accepting?'

  Example: 'I shouldn't feel this way', 'This shouldn't be happening to me'.

- **Make a choice:** Acceptance or Non-Acceptance

  You have the power to select your response according to the situation at hand. If the situation

(continued)

(continued)

can be altered or affected positively without unacceptable consequences, this is your chance to make a change. On the other hand, if the situation is unchangeable or altering creates more issues, and your choices boil down to either: embracing it or struggling against it (aware this may lead you to further distress).

Using this technique of acceptance, your response will trigger new thoughts and new emotions, and this will expand your reality. Soon, you will find yourself in a different present tense that supports your higher vibrational frequency.

Thoughts and Reflections

Finding acceptance, or better yet, trying to find even the smallest ounce of contentment or gratitude in the present moment, will navigate your pursuit of luck with greater awareness and authenticity. See that true fulfilment lies not in external accomplishments but in the inside journey of self-discovery and connection to ourselves and others.

Once you ditch the *'I'll be happy when'* bullshit and become realigned with what will bring you lasting luck –

That's where the magic happens.

That's where your manifestations come into play.

That's where your luck changes.

Be in the moment, right now and accept how you're feeling. A minute from now, you'll breathe easier. An hour from now, you'll reframe. A day from now, you'll relax. A year from now, you will be in a completely different place, surrounded by different energies and different people, doing different things, with different goals, ideas, dreams, and plans.

So enjoy now – you will never have this moment again. I know you may be anxious or overwhelmed, but there is something to be found in the time you are living. Focus on that and savour it because . . .

A present, accepting attitude and profound gratitude create Lucky Girl magnitude.

Make this your rallying battle cry to seriously step up your game. Follow this rule, Lucky Girl, and just watch your luck change.

8

It's Time to Get Lucky . . .

Congratulations! You've reached the end of this book, but the start of your Lucky Girl Life is only just beginning!

This moment serves as the pot of gold gleaming at the end of your Lucky Girl rainbow.

As you've arrived at this final chapter, I hope you've realised that luck is not solely about random chance. It's more than just winning a lottery or chancing upon a four-leaf clover; it can take various forms, depending on your perspective.

The case studies, scientific insights, and lessons within these pages provide a solid foundation but can only get you so far. The torch is now passed to you to elevate your luck to the next level. Crafting your own luck might seem like a monumental endeavour and overwhelming task, but armed with the right mindset, attitude, and actions, you possess the internal tools to achieve greatness.

By incorporating the key principles outlined in this book, you can significantly enhance your prospects of life and attract good fortune across various areas. Removing those blocks and limiting beliefs, allow these newfound learnings to pour out into every aspect of your life, becoming:

Lucky in Life

Lucky in Love

Lucky in Line of Work

From altering your perspective and shifting your mindset to revamping your daily rituals and routines and constructing realistic plans for your aspirations, whether you choose to take a single insight learned or adopt them all, let these pearls of wisdom serve as guides towards creating lasting change and making tangible strides towards your objectives, desires, and Lucky Girl Goals.

While some associate luck with being in the right place at the right time, consider what would happen if you could engineer circumstances in your favour? This is precisely where the concept of Lucky Girl Syndrome comes into play.

And who knows, perhaps you'll come to realise that all the power to truly embody the essence of a Lucky Girl already lies inside of you.

Let's press play on Life's playlist. Alexa: Play 'Get Lucky' by Daft Punk.

Here we go . . .

Surrender

The thought of surrendering might appear counterintuitive at first glance.

The art of Lucky Girl Syndrome revolves around the skill of clearly defining one's desires and welcoming them into reality. An often-overlooked facet of successful manifestation is the practice of surrendering and releasing the compulsion to micromanage every aspect of the process. This is because being overly fixated on specific outcomes can generate stress and disappointment, causing a disruption in the smooth flow of positive energy.

Let's illustrate this principle in the context of seeking love. Imagine you're on a quest for your perfect romantic partner – someone who resonates deeply with your soul. As you embark on finding them, of course, you may want to set your intention for love and genuine connection, but it's equally vital to surrender to the notion that the right companion will come into your life at precisely the opportune moment. This surrender allows you to relinquish control and trust in the natural unfolding of events, enabling the manifestation process to occur organically and harmoniously.

Surrender; don't settle.

When it comes to your Lucky Girl Goals, regardless of their nature, settling should never be on the table. Instead, envision your goal as an exhilarating investment in yourself and your future. Just as you wouldn't settle for mediocrity in investments that have the potential to yield substantial returns, don't compromise on your aspirations and dreams. Approach your goals with the same determination and enthusiasm that you would bring to a wise financial investment. By doing so, you ensure that you're giving yourself the best possible chance to manifest your desires and achieve the success you're aiming for.

Surrendering to luck involves letting go of rigid expectations and allowing the natural flow of opportunities and outcomes to guide you. It's about trusting the process and being open to unexpected possibilities while maintaining a positive outlook and taking proactive steps.

Allow your internal dialogue to quieten, granting your intuitive self the stage to speak. If the messages remain elusive, give yourself permission to let go. The act of surrendering often paves the way for clarity and revelation.

Surrender the need for constant control and allow the universe to play its role.

Get Ready

Brace yourself, people, because we are soon about to land into luck.

You've read the book, but the learning doesn't stop here.

Use knowledge learned throughout these pages and apply it in your everyday Lucky Life and just watch as opportunities and success start flooding in. Remember, knowledge is power, but it's the application of that knowledge that truly brings about positive change. So go out there and make the most of your newfound wisdom!

Go back to your Lucky Girl Guide (see Chapter 3 and Appendix 1) and the Debrief exercises throughout this book time and time again.

By consistently revisiting, you will become more adept at identifying and overcoming any lingering limiting beliefs. Just like a skilled tennis player, you will be able to swiftly bat them away, allowing your newfound wisdom to guide you towards a life filled with endless opportunities and success. So keep honing your knowledge and applying it fearlessly, for it is through this continuous effort that true positive change can be achieved. Declutter your life. Implement new habits learned and promote personal growth and self-care. Embrace opportunities for self-reflection and continuous improvement.

Make full use the 'I'm Sure' method – and get ready to let that luck flow right in!

Realistic Positivity

Luck, laws of manifestation, and attraction is all about being positive.

Lucky Girls possess a flexible mindset, allowing room for experimentation and unshakable confidence in their intuition. It's like embarking on an exciting adventure where you embrace opportunities while being realistic.

Approaching luck with a positive outlook involves embracing the unknown with optimism. You take calculated risks and venture out of your comfort zone, fully aware that not every step will be smooth. This attitude aligns with Lucky Girl's willingness to take leaps of faith, acknowledging the potential pitfalls but still believing in the possibility of success.

Prepare

If you can embrace the reality that life doesn't always unfold as you wish, then you will see the beauty that lies therein. If everything followed a scripted path, growth would be stunted and learning would cease, and *how boring would life be if it were that way?*

Be prepared for the good, the bad, the ugly, and the fabulous to come your way.

Preparation is a major factor in navigating life's uncertainties. And realism is pivotal in preparation.

To mitigate the impact of 'bad luck', a blend of preparation and strategic thinking is required. Just as you actively invite good luck into your life, a proactive mindset can help soften the blows of bad luck. Begin with manageable steps, focusing on factors you can control rather than dwelling on unlikely scenarios. Utilise the tools provided in this book and let your Lucky Girl Goals Guide serve as your BFF to success.

Being prepared means being open-minded and willing to see things from different perspectives. This allows you to see opportunities that others might overlook, and it can help you discover new paths towards your goals. Be open to feedback and suggestions and learn from your mistakes. When you cultivate an open-minded attitude, you'll be more adaptable to change and more willing to take calculated risks.

Countless opportunities are scattered around us like hidden gems waiting to be discovered. The challenge lies in our awareness of them. Many of us go about our routines, seldom realising the potential that surrounds us.

Lucky Girl Syndrome responds to your energy, but it also values your efforts. Actively put yourself in situations that amplify your chances of getting lucky. This might involve stepping outside your comfort zone and into new experiences, trying out different activities, or connecting with people who share your passions. The more you immerse yourself in the currents of life, the more opportunities you'll create to magnetise your luck.

If it wasn't for the Wright brothers, who would have thought a metal tube in the sky could take you from one side of the world to another?

You don't need to create the next world-breaking, revolutionary invention, you need to create a life that exceeds your needs. The lucky ones have long-term goals because it helps them identify opportunities that best align with their mission when they come knocking,

Opportunity is your guide to lead you into uncharted territories, unexpected encounters, and connections. A helping hand to meet your Lucky Girl Goal.

Curiosity extends beyond personal growth; it's a dynamic force that can attract luck and serendipity into your life, akin to opening a treasure chest of possibilities. When you're genuinely curious about the world around you, you open yourself up to a myriad of opportunities and experiences that might otherwise have remained hidden.

Capturing your surroundings inquisitively increases the likelihood of stumbling upon situations that align with your desires. The act of exploring, questioning, and seeking understanding becomes a catalyst where each interaction, each new piece of information, becomes a potential stepping stone towards your Lucky Girl Goals. The world becomes your playground, ripe with chances waiting to be seized. As you explore, question, and engage, you not only expand your horizons but also attract the lucky coincidences that enrich your life's experience.

Act like an alien – approach each day with the wonder of a child, eager to explore, learn, and make connections.

Allow your curiosity to guide you, and watch as the universe responds by unveiling a world of opportunities you might have never imagined.

Seize unexpected opportunities, break away from the monotony of routine, and occasionally summon the bravery to relinquish control. The world is brimming with chances for those Lucky Girls willing to embrace them.

Radically Resilient

You are a strong, courageous, badass, Lucky Girl.

You've been through tough times, but you got back up each and every time.

How do I know this about you?

Because you are here, reading this now! Because you are: *radically resilient*.

Even in the darkest moments, when it feels like the world is crumbling, there always exists a transformative potential.

Always ask yourself in times of struggle: *What is the lesson from this bad luck? Has this awful experience taught me something/anything?*

Life's trajectory may seem like an unending spiral of challenges for you, but amid such trials, be open to the possibility that setbacks and disappointments are not the end; they are mere waypoints in a much grander voyage. If a venture falters, people let you down, you lose out, you get heartbroken – it's all sh*t, but if you muster the courage to start anew, then you, my friend, are **resilient.**

Challenges become your crucible of strength. The adversities that knock you down don't define you; your ability to rise from them does. Lucky Girl, you can transmute bad luck into luck.

Let laughter become your armour, shake off setbacks as your art form, and persist in your anthem. Each day brings another chance to recommence, to rekindle the flame of determination. If your plan falters, know that perhaps that endeavour isn't futile. Rather, it's for learning and refinement. Failure isn't the verdict on your ideas; it's an invitation to fine-tune your approach.

Rise stronger each time. Endure, adapt, and transcend, Lucky Girl.

Guided by Goodness

Do whatever it is that makes you feel damn good. Work these good feelings into your life more often, even if it's just for a few minutes. In time, you'll start to notice that, overall, you feel more positive and healthy and more likely to be on the receiving end of good luck as a result.

Relish that sensation of goodness; it's a subtle yet profound elevation of your energy. It's this upliftment that holds harmonisation to manifestation and your daily existence. Tune into these feelings more frequently, even if only for brief moments. Over time, you'll witness a transformation – an overall surge of positivity and vitality. And, remarkably, this surge can attract not only personal well-being but also the blessings of good luck.

Just a few minutes spent in a pleasurable pursuit or engaging in an activity that resonates deeply with your soul, these instances of good serve as markers of alignment with your desires. Consistently engaging in activities that feel good to you, you're creating a steady current of positivity that nourishes you and your manifestations.

As you immerse yourself in the sea of joy, you're naturally drawn to a more positive state of being. This shift in your energetic frequency has the potential to attract more favourable circumstances. The universe responds to the energy you emit, and your increased positivity becomes a magnetic force that aligns with similar energies.

The ripple effect doesn't stop at your own experience; it extends to the world around you. Just as you seek to attract luck for yourself, extending that sense of goodness to others forms a feedback loop of positivity. Acts of kindness, no matter how small, are like pebbles creating waves of positivity in the ocean of life. The positive energy you radiate amplifies the collective vibration, creating an atmosphere conducive to the manifestation of luck and blessings.

Lucky Girl, remember that what feels good for you is also an offering to the universe. Aligning with activities and experiences that elevate your vibration is a deliberate step towards living in harmony with your intentions. As you experience the swell of positivity, it's not just your own reality that benefits, it's the interconnectedness of all things.

Give a Sh*t without Giving a Sh*t

Newsflash: People will always have opinions about what you do, no matter what you do.

You can't control that, so don't let it control you.

Wasting your energy on worrying about what others might be saying behind your back is a one-way ticket to misery.

Let's break it down: everyone's got their own lives to live and their own issues to deal with. Trust me, they're not lying awake at night thinking about your every move. They're too wrapped up in their own drama to give you more than a passing thought. It's not about you; it's about them.

So here's a challenge for you: shift your focus from playing detective on what others might be saying, to concentrating on what truly matters – your growth, dreams, and well-being. If you keep measuring your worth by other people's opinions, you're setting yourself up for a never-ending cycle of disappointment.

Your luck is about you, not them. The sooner you embrace that, the lighter your heart will be. So chin up, face forward, and let the naysayers chatter away. You've got more important things to do and a brighter path to step onto.

Watch Your Mouth

Pay heed to your verbal expressions; you take control of the energy you project into the universe by positioning your words with your intentions.

Make your words harmonious with your actions – an alliance between what you say and what you do. This congruence creates a resonance that ripples through your manifestations, amplifying their impact.

Lucky Girls are kind, compassionate, healthy, positive, open, and flowing.

These aren't limited to external interactions; they start within. When you nurture your voice, you set the stage for the manifestation of self-belief and genuine luck. Self-love isn't self-indulgence; it's a cornerstone of empowerment.

Supporting others on their unique paths is a reflection of the luck you've acquired. Offering compassionate words to those around you not only uplifts them but also contributes to the collective energy. It's a recognition that your language isn't just a tool for personal manifestations but a means to create ripples of positivity that touch lives.

In Lucky Girl Syndrome, every word is a note that contributes to the overall harmony. As you watch your words, know that they have the power to sculpt your reality and the reality of others. This holistic approach to language isn't just about attracting luck; it's about co-creating a world where manifestations align with authenticity, empathy, and positive change.

Avoid perpetuating stereotypes or engaging in discriminatory behaviours. Treat others with respect and empathy, regardless of their background.

Reflect on your own biases and prejudices. We all have biases, but being aware of them can help you challenge and overcome them. Work on your self-improvement and growth in this regard.

Trust

Unquestionably, place your trust in your intuition.

At the risk of sounding like Captain Hindsight – if I were given a pound for each time myself or a close friend shared, *'I could sense deep within that something wasn't right, but charged ahead anyway'*, I'd certainly be a very wealthy lady.

Trust, both in yourself and the universe, forms an unshakable foundation in the pursuit of attracting luck.

Your gut is your most steadfast advisor – containing more wisdom and insight than you could imagine.

How many times have you ignored the subtle but powerful feeling in your core? These thoughts of '*I knew it wasn't right*', fluttery sensations, and whispers of intuition hold potent messages that deserve our attention.

When your inner voice seems drowned out, create space for quiet introspection. Amid the hustle of life, sometimes the most profound guidance is found in the hush of stillness. The notion of destiny assumes a prominent role; what's meant to be will inevitably find its way to you.

Believe in divine timing and alleviate the pressure to control every outcome. Trusting the process and trusting yourself become intertwined as you recognise that your instincts are finely attuned to the cosmic rhythm.

Trust isn't confined to the self; it extends to the universe itself. Embrace the unwavering belief that the universe is conspiring in your favour. This deep-seated faith bolsters your journey, showing every twist and turn serves a purpose, and ultimately leads to a positive outcome. This trust in the universe's benevolence magnifies your resonance with positivity and luck.

When things don't go your way, follow the '*Burnt Toast Theory*'. The idea is that if you burn your toast in the morning (aka something challenging or bad luck appears), the time you spend making another toast may have saved you from a car accident on your morning commute, or maybe your toast makes you late for your first meeting, but as you walk into the office, you meet that someone special, which you wouldn't have done if you didn't burn the damn toast! With this theory you reframe sh*t situations and failures better and lean into the idea that the universe has your back. Trusting that everything happens for a reason, or that moments of lack mean something better is on its way.

Believe

Your faith in your abilities and talents serves as a magnetic force, drawing prosperity and luck towards you.

Convinced of your capacity to influence your destiny, you start to create your luck. The foundational step is to nurture an unwavering belief in your inherent potential. Encompass yourself with a cocoon of affirmations that kindle your inner fire, motivational quotes that ignite your spirit, and individuals who amplify your confidence.

When your self-belief shines brightly within, every challenge morphs into an opportunity. You perceive potential where others see obstacles. This newfound perspective propels you to take decisive action, converting your aspirations into tangible realities.

Be around Others Who Believe in You

Reflect on those who radiate a contagiously vibrant energy, like a lucky charm personified. Their presence uplifts and elevates; their positive outlook is infectious. They possess a remarkable knack for spotting and celebrating the goodness that abounds – in the world, in others, and in themselves. This ability not only amplifies their own luck but also transforms the atmosphere around them.

Be Patient

Have patience, Lucky Girl, for what you desire is on its way.

Patience isn't merely a virtue; it's a practice of both trust and surrender. As you wait for your aspirations to come to fruition, remember the timing they symbolise. Accept the mindset of your forebears, appreciate what is, and find solace in the belief that life's timing is impeccable. Your dreams, like the seasons, have their own cadence. Trust in this rhythm, and in due course, the universe will present you with the beautiful symphony of your desires fulfilled.

Receive

'Infinite receiving' embodies the profound concept of being open and receptive to the endless flow of abundance, love, and opportunities that the universe has to offer. It's about understanding that the more you give, the more you receive, and that there is an unlimited reservoir of blessings available to you.

It means acknowledging and appreciating the blessings, both big and small, that come your way.

It involves letting go of limitations, fears, and doubts, allowing yourself to be a vessel for the universe's abundant gifts.

When you embrace the idea of infinite receiving, you invite positivity and abundance into your life. It's not just about material wealth but also about receiving love, kindness, wisdom, and experiences. By acknowledging the abundance around you and being open to receive, you create a positive energy flow that attracts even more blessings into your life.

The universe is infinitely abundant, and there is no limit to what you can receive when your heart is open and your spirit is aligned with the energy of abundance. Embrace the concept of infinite receiving and watch as your life and luck becomes beautifully entwined with blessings beyond measure.

Say Thank You

Good manners in exchange for all the good you receive.

Genuinely expressing thanks for the blessings we already possess and sending out vibrations of appreciation that magnetise positive energies to us. Gratitude isn't solely about acknowledging tangible possessions; it also enables us to perceive intangible gifts and reframe challenges as opportunities. Something sh*t happens? There are always lessons in bad luck, so say thank you, even if it's a sarcastic 'Oh, thanks a lot', you're still giving the universe what it wants: gratitude.

This shift in perspective creates a positive feedback loop where focusing on the good attracts more of it, perpetuating the cycle of positivity. Align intentions with the cosmic currents of positivity through gratitude, invite opportunities and experiences that resonate with our desires, and let in luck.

Stay Present

Remember the golden rule:

A present, accepting attitude and profound gratitude create Lucky Girl magnitude.

Aka, living in the now.

Being fully in the present moment is the greatest gift you could ever give yourself. It's a gift that you should never return or take for granted.

Without it, you're letting life pass you by. Life has a tendency to slip past you unnoticed. It's as if you're merely a bystander, observing life's unfolding without actively participating in its beauty. Life continues to move, irrespective of whether you're fully engaged or not. The moments that hold the potential to transform your life and bring luck your way might pass you by if you're not attentive to them. A lack of awareness can inadvertently lead to closed doors and missed opportunities, leaving you wondering why luck seems elusive.

Being present is not just a practice but a profound way of life, a conscious choice to embrace each moment with open arms. In doing so, you create a space where luck and serendipity naturally gravitate, enriching your existence. This approach to life ensures that you don't just exist on the sidelines but actively participate in the grand scheme of experiences in life, where each note represents an opportunity waiting to be seized. Being present, you craft a life that is not only lived but truly lived to the fullest.

Actually Take Action

Finally, Lucky Girl, it's time to take a definitive step forward – a step that will elevate your manifestations beyond mere intentions. Lucky Girl Syndrome isn't just about envisioning your dreams; it's about actively participating and showing up. So, gather your courage, grab your LG Guide because it's time to move with purpose and intention.

As you stand at the crossroads of intention and realisation, understand that all emotions, including fear and doubt, are natural companions. But don't let them dictate your course. Luck favours the bold, the courageous, and those who dare to leap even in the face of uncertainty. The path to your dreams might seem daunting, but each step you take with unwavering determination bridges the gap between your desires and your reality.

The catalyst for luck requires venturing beyond what you deem comfortable. Luck isn't just about chance; it's about being willing to take risks, no matter how big or small. Each risk you take propels you forward, opening doors you never knew existed.

Action is the law's call. The universe responds to your energy, but it's your actions that set the course. Embrace the concept of proactive participation – the idea that you hold the reins of your destiny. Don't wait for opportunities to knock on your door; create them for yourself. By stepping out of the passenger seat and into the driver's seat, you amplify your power to generate luck.

Aligned action helps you make decisions that are in harmony with your long-term vision. You become more present in your actions, savouring the journey rather than just focusing on the destination.

Engaging in activities that align with your passions and values brings a deep sense of fulfilment. When you're passionate about what you're doing, your enthusiasm becomes a powerful driving force.

When your actions are aligned with your purpose, you're more likely to persevere in the face of challenges; you'll be more explicit on next steps and more efficient and effective in your efforts. Your determination comes from a genuine belief in what you're doing, eliminating feelings of being stuck or indecisiveness.

In essence, aligned action is about being true to yourself and living a life that reflects your authentic desires. It's a powerful way to navigate the complexities of luck, ensuring that every step you take is purposeful, meaningful, and in harmony with your innermost beliefs and dreams.

Imagine any action as planting seeds in the soil of possibility, nurturing them with intention, and watching them blossom into fortunate outcomes.

Networking, for instance, forms a bridge between our aspirations and the world of opportunity. Engaging with a diverse array of individuals allows us to tap into a treasure trove of insights, collaborations, and synergies that can lead to extraordinary breakthroughs. Each connection made and each conversation held is like adding another piece to the puzzle of possibility.

The key is not to be a passive recipient of luck but an active seeker. If you are waiting for luck to knock on your door, you may as well wait for rain in the Atacama Desert (*FYI, no rainfall has been recorded in the last 500 years!*). Instead, we must step boldly forward and actively court it. Proactivity propels us from the sidelines onto the stage of opportunity, where we can act with the rhythms of change and transformation.

You are the proactive architect of your own luck. Venture out and unlock potentials to luck that were once hidden. Always take aligned action with a heart full of courage and a spirit determined to transform dreams of luck into reality.

Yay – I Got Lucky Girl, Now What?

You've reached a point that once seemed distant and ethereal – the realisation of your manifested dreams. The universe has conspired to bring your intentions to life, and now you stand amidst the very manifestations that once occupied your thoughts and hopes. As you bask in the glory of your achievements, it's only natural to wonder, *'Ok - I got lucky, and now I have everything I manifested . . . now what?'*

Keep Going

While attaining your manifested desires is a cause for celebration, the journey is far from over. Manifestation isn't a one-time event, but a continuous process of evolving desires and aspirations. Harness this momentum to set new intentions, channel your creativity, and embark on fresh quests.

Ride the Cycle

Just as the moon waxes and wanes, so does the cycle of fulfilment. Acknowledge that life is a dynamic interplay of ups and downs, successes, and challenges. Understanding this ebb and flow, maintaining a balanced perspective, and appreciating both the moments of manifestation and the times of introspection. Allow these experiences to enrich your soul and nurture your growth.

Share the Love

Your success story can inspire and uplift those around you. The power of Lucky Girl isn't just in realising your desires but also in the positive influence it can have on others. Share your story, the lessons you've learned, and the techniques that have worked or not worked for you. Your insights might be the catalyst for someone else's transformative experience.

Help Create a Lucky World

With Lucky Girl, comes the responsibility to contribute to the greater good. As you revel in your achievements, contemplate how you can extend your impact beyond yourself. Consider aligning your manifestations with endeavours that benefit your community, society, or the environment. Use your luck and abundance to drive positive change, and create a legacy that far surpasses personal achievements.

Stay Lucky

In the rush to pursue new aspirations, it's easy to forget the significance of gratitude and mindfulness. Pause to acknowledge the hurdles you've overcome and the gifts you've received.

Gratitude amplifies your positive energy, attracting even more abundance into your life. Stay present, relishing the experiences that accompany your manifestations.

Life is full of unexpected twists and turns, even for the luckiest among us. It will never go as smoothly as we plan, and as progress isn't linear either, it's essential to extract wisdom from our lows to ascend to greater heights.

Thoughts and Reflections

With this book coming to a close, I hope you have expanded your horizons and identified areas where you may have been going wrong while unearthing novel avenues to usher in fortune, possibilities, opportunities, and, above all, luck.

Luck isn't solely a roll of the dice. It's an amalgamation and alchemy of courage, focus, and a willingness to experiment. It's all about declaring to the world: *'Dear future, I'm ready.'* and then following up that intention with actionable steps, hard work, and unrelenting effort to meet your goals.

This is a friendly reminder that your luck will come. Be patient. Life is not a race, so slow down. It's OK to start over time and time again. It's OK to change the course of your path. It's never too late.

Your time will come, Lucky Girl.

Take a second to acknowledge that you have one life, and how you deem luck and create it is up to you. Soak that in. Internalise this concept.

Take risks, follow your happiness, and make the most of your one and only shot at this life.

As you stand at the precipice of your manifested dreams, remember that this is merely a chapter in the expansive book of your life. Embrace the cycle of manifestation, from intention-setting to realisation and beyond. By sharing your luck, contributing to the world's betterment, and remaining in a state of gratitude, you perpetuate the dance of manifestation – a dance that, when performed with authenticity and purpose, shapes a life of profound satisfaction and meaningful impact, clearing the path for you to walk the Lucky Girl walk.

Luck is a harmonious interplay of your actions, intentions, and the universe's benevolence, coalescing to shape your reality. Unlock a symphony of endless possibilities, leading to a life where luck is no longer a distant wish, but a vibrant reality crafted by your own hands.

Embody a Lucky Girl, and show up as her each and every day, you'll find that luck isn't just chance it's a mindset, a way of being. It's in the gratitude you carry for the small joys, the resilience you show in the face of challenges, and the kindness you spread to others. Embrace the moments of serendipity, but also recognise the power within you to create your own luck through hard work, positivity, and an unwavering belief in yourself.

Being a Lucky Girl isn't about avoiding difficulties; it's about facing them with courage and grace, knowing that every obstacle is an opportunity in disguise. It's about seeing the silver linings, learning from setbacks, and believing that setbacks are merely setups for a comeback.

When you're living authentically, you inspire others to do the same. Being a Lucky Girl, you'll inspire others to find their own luck too. Your optimism will be contagious, your smile will be genuine, and your spirit will be unbreakable. Remember, luck is not just about what happens to you; it's about how you respond to what happens. So, wear your luck like a crown, and let it radiate from within, illuminating your path and brightening the world around you.

What are you waiting for, Lucky Girl?

Your life of luck awaits.

Notes

Chapter 1

1. Duckworth, A. L., Peterson, C., Matthews, M. D., & Kelly, D. R. (2007). Grit: Perseverance and passion for long-term goals. *Journal of Personality and Social Psychology*, 92(6), 1087–1101.

2. Dweck, C. S. (2006). *Mindset: The new psychology of success*. Random House.

Chapter 2

1. Shermer, M., & Menton, D. N. (2006). The Secret: The Law of Attraction—It's Not All Wishful Thinking. *Skeptic*, 12(4), 28–37.

2. Gressier, E. (2010). The effects of mental imagery on motor skill acquisition and performance: A randomized controlled study on a fine motor skill task. *Journal of Sports Science & Medicine*, 9(3), 413-419.

3. Wiseman, R., Watt, C., Greening, E., O'Keeffe, C., & Smith, F. (2016). Does the law of attraction affect academic performance or creative output? A large-scale experimental test. *Thinking & Reasoning*, 23(2), 115-132.

4. Lyubomirsky, S., King, L. A., & Diener, E. (2005). The benefits of frequent positive affect: Does happiness lead to success? *Psychological Bulletin*, 131(6), 803–855.

5. Weiner, B. (1985). An attributional theory of achievement motivation and emotion. *Psychological Review*, 92(4), 548–573.

6. Bandura, A. (1997). *Self-Efficacy: The Exercise of Control*. W.H. Freeman and Company.

7. Peterson, C., Semmel, A., von Baeyer, C., Abramson, L. Y., Metalsky, G. I., & Seligman, M. E. P. (1982). The attributional style questionnaire. *Cognitive Therapy and Research*, 6(3), 287–299.

8. Carver, C. S., Scheier, M. F., & Segerstrom, S. C. (2010). Optimism. *Clinical Psychology Review*, 30(7), 879–889.

9. Pellegrino, A., Abe, M., & Shannon, R. (2022). The dark side of social media: Content effects on the relationship between materialism and consumption behaviors. *Frontiers in Psychology*, 13, 870614. doi: 10.3389/fpsyg.2022.870614

Chapter 3

1. Petrie (Director). (2006). *Just My Luck* [Film]. Regency Enterprises.

2. Zemeckis, R. (Director). (1994). *Forrest Gump* [Film]. Paramount Pictures.

3. Duckworth, A. L., Milkman, K. L., & Laibson, D. (2018). Beyond willpower: Strategies for reducing failures of self-control. *Psychological Science in the Public Interest*, 19(3), 102–129. DOI: 10.1177/1529100618821893

4. Gollwitzer, P. M., & Sheeran, P. (2006). Implementation intentions and goal achievement: A meta-analysis of effects and processes. In M. P. Zanna (Ed.), *Advances in Experimental Social Psychology*, Vol. 38, pp. 69–119). Elsevier Academic Press. https://doi.org/10.1016/S0065-2601(06)38002-1

Chapter 4

1. Lee, J. Y., & Kim, J. (2022). Excessive self-healing and mental health: A paradoxical relationship. *Frontiers in Psychology*, 13, Article 122.

Chapter 5

1. Mullainathan, S., & Shafir, E. (2013). *Scarcity: Why Having Too Little Means So Much*. New York, NY: Times Books.

2. Rosenthal, R., & Jacobson, L. (1968). *Pygmalion in the Classroom: Teacher Expectation and Pupils' Intellectual Development*. New York, NY: Holt, Rinehart, and Winston.

3. Fardouly, J., Diedrichs, P. C., Vartanian, L. R., & Halliwell, E. (2015). Social comparisons on social media: the impact of Facebook on young women's body image concerns and mood. *Body Image*, 13, 38–45.

4. Krasnova, H., Wenninger, H., Widjaja, T., & Buxmann, P. (2015). Envy on Facebook: A Hidden Threat to Users' Life Satisfaction? In Proceedings of the 33rd Annual ACM Conference on Human Factors in Computing Systems (pp. 1393–1402).

5. Stoeber, J. (2015). Exploring the role of perfectionism in the context of professional athletes. *Journal of Sport Psychology*, 36(3), 249-262.

6. Brooks, A. (2014). Luck and the entrepreneurial mind. *Harvard Business Review*, 92(7-8), 60–69.

7. Gabriel, M., & Goldberg, E. (Directors). (1995). Pocahontas [Motion Picture]. Walt Disney Pictures.

8. Russ, S. W. (2004). Play, creativity, and adaptive functioning: Implications for play interventions. *Journal of Applied School Psychology*, 20(1), 29-48.

9. Milne, A. A. (1926). *Winnie-the-Pooh*. E. P. Dutton.

Chapter 6

1. Blakemore, S. J., Bristow, L. C., Bird, G., Frith, C. D., & Ward, J. (2012). The role of motor mimicry in social interaction. *Social Cognitive and Affective Neuroscience*, 7(1), 49–54.

2. Smyth, J. M., Johnson, J. A., Auer, B. J., Lehman, E., Talamo, G., & Sciamanna, C. N. (2018). Online positive affect journaling

in the improvement of mental distress and well-being in general medical patients with elevated anxiety symptoms: A preliminary randomized controlled trial. *Journal of Anxiety Disorders*, 57, 32–40.

3. Fredrickson, B. L. (2001). The Role of Positive Emotions in Positive Psychology: The Broaden-and-Build Theory of Positive Emotions. *American Psychologist*, 56(3), 218–226. PMCID: PMC3122271. PMID: 11315248. [Available in PMC 2011 Jun 24].

4. Matthews, G. (2015). Goal setting: A review of research and practical implications. *Applied Psychology*, 64(1), 1–19.

5. Clay, R. A., & Crocker, J. (2006). Affirmation and social behavior. In M. P. Zanna (Ed.), Advances in experimental social psychology (Vol. 38, pp. 1-78). Academic Press.

6. Legare, C. H., Strauss, B., & Crocker, J. (2010). Self-affirmation reduces cognitive dissonance and enhances problem-solving. *Journal of Personality and Social Psychology*, 98(3), 467–479.

7. Creswell, J. D., Dutcher, J. M., Klein, W. M. P., Harris, P. R., & Levine, J. M. (2013). Self-affirmation improves problem-solving under stress. PLOS ONE, 8(5), e62593.

8. Kosslyn, S. M., Ganis, G., & Thompson, W. L. (2001). Neural foundations of imagery. *Nature Reviews Neuroscience*, 2(9), 635–642.

9. Schredl, M., & Erlacher, D. (2011). Lucid dreaming and visualization: A new approach to enhance self-efficacy? *Dreaming: Journal of the Association for the Study of Dreams*, 21(1), 55–68.

10. Mulder, T., Zijlstra, F. R. H., Van der Kamp, J., & Rikkert, M. J. P. M. (2004). The role of motor imagery in the rehabilitation of arm function after stroke: A systematic review of the literature. *Journal of Rehabilitation Medicine*, 36(5), 222–239.

11. Fredrickson, B. L. (2001). The role of positive emotions in positive psychology: The broaden-and-build theory of positive emotions. *American Psychologist*, 56(3), 218–226.

12. Beck, A. T. (1979). *Cognitive Therapy and the Emotional Disorders*. New York: Penguin Books.

13. Domhoff, G. W. (2005). Reframing the classical clinical problem of impaired dream recall: A restatement of the confluence model of dreaming. *Psychological Bulletin*, 131(2), 202–217.

14. LaBerge, S. (1990). Lucid dreaming: Psychophysiological studies of consciousness during REM sleep. In R. R. Bootzen, J. F. Kihlstrom, & D. L. Schacter (Eds.), *Implicit Memory and Metacognition* (pp. 198–214). Lawrence Erlbaum Associates.

15. Lyubomirsky, S., Sheldon, K. M., & Schkade, D. (2005). Pursuing happiness: The architecture of sustainable change. *Review of General Psychology*, 9(2), 111-131.

16. Lyubomirsky, S., Sheldon, K. M., & Schkade, D. (2008). Pursuing happiness: The architecture of sustainable well-being. *Psychological Science*, 19(9), 961–968.

17. Curtis, Richard. 2003. Love Actually. United States: Universal Pictures.

18. Mecca Bingo. (2023). How superstitious is the UK? Retrieved from https://blog.meccabingo.com/how-superstitious-is-the-uk/

19. High Performance Institute. (2023, August 4). Self-control, high performance and the limits of willpower. Retrieved from https://www.highperformanceinstitute.com/blog/self-control-high-performance-and-the-limits-of-willpower

20. Saxbe, D. E., Repetti, R., & Graesch, A. P. (2011). Time spent in home and neighborhood settings: A full-day exploration. *Journal of Family Psychology*, 25(6), 915–927.

21. Uzzi, B., & Spiro, J. (2005). Collaboration and creativity: The small world problem. *American Journal of Sociology*, 111(2), 447–504.

22. Liu, C. (2023). A normative theory of luck. Frontiers in Psychology, Section: *Organizational Psychology*, 14, Article 1157527. https://doi.org/10.3389/fpsyg.2023.1157527

23. Emmons, R. A., & McCullough, M. E. (2003). Counting blessings versus burdens: An experimental investigation of gratitude and subjective well-being in daily life. *Journal of Personality and Social Psychology*, 84(2), 377–389.

Chapter 7

1. Diener, E. (2006). Guidelines for national indicators of subjective well-being and ill-being. *Journal of Happiness Studies*, 7(4), 397–404.

2. Brickman, P., Coates, D., & Janoff-Bulman, R. (1978). Lottery winners and accident victims: Is happiness relative? *Journal of Personality and Social Psychology*, 36(8), 917–927.

3. Ben-Shahar, T. (2007). *Happier: Learn the Secrets to Daily Joy and Lasting Fulfillment*. McGraw-Hill Education.

4. Huffington, A. (2014). *Thrive: The Third Metric to Redefining Success and Creating a Life of Well-Being, Wisdom, and Wonder.* Harmony.

5. Diener, E., & Biswas-Diener, R. (2008). *Happiness: Unlocking the Mysteries of Psychological Wealth.* Blackwell Publishing.

6. Roemer, L., & Orsillo, S. M. (2002). Expanding our conceptualization of and treatment for generalized anxiety disorder: Integrating mindfulness/acceptance-based approaches with existing cognitive-behavioral models. *Clinical Psychology: Science and Practice*, 9(1), 54–68.

7. Kashdan, T. B., & Breen, W. E. (2007). Materialism and diminished well-being: Experiential avoidance as a mediating mechanism. *Journal of Social and Clinical Psychology*, 26(5), 521–539.

8. Harris, R. (2007). Acceptance and Commitment Therapy (ACT) Introductory Workshop Handout. Retrieved from https://www.actmindfully.com.au

9. Khoury, B., Lecomte, T., Fortin, G., Masse, M., Therien, P., Bouchard, V., . . . & Hofmann, S. G. (2013). Mindfulness-based therapy: A comprehensive meta-analysis. *Clinical Psychology Review*, 33(6), 763–771.

10. Tolle, E. (1997). *The Power of Now: A Guide to Spiritual Enlightenment.* New World Library.

Appendix 1: Lucky Girl Goals Guide

Step 1: Lucky Girl Goal		
Step 2: Prepare				
Step 3: Opportunities				
Step 4: Potential				

Step 5: Mindset					
Step 6: Action					
Step 7: Learn					
Step 8: Celebrate					

Appendix 2: Lucky Girl Affirmations

- The universe puts me in the right place at the right time.

- I am a magnet for good luck and positive opportunities.

- I am open to receiving unexpected blessings and fortunate events.

- I trust in the universe's abundant flow of luck that comes my way.

- I am aligned with the energy of luck

- Opportunities for luck and success are drawn to me like a magnet.

- Every day is a blessing. Every day is a lesson.

- Luck is a constant companion, guiding me towards my dreams.

- I am grateful for the lucky breaks and serendipitous moments in my life.

- I deserve to experience luck.

- I am the architect of my own luck, creating a life filled with abundance.

- I radiate positivity and luck, creating a ripple effect of good fortune.

- Luck gravitates naturally towards me.

- My intentions and actions align with the flow of luck

- I release any resistance to luck and allow it to flow into my life.

- With each breath, I am inhaling luck and exhaling gratitude.

Appendix 3: Website Resources

www.lucky-collective.com/

In the journey of life, we all encounter moments when we could use a little extra support, guidance, or simply a moment of peace. In *Lucky Girl*, we've explored the power of luck, the importance of living in the present moment, and the transformative effects of practices like EFT (Emotional Freedom Techniques) tapping and meditation. If you're looking to dive deeper into these practices or seek additional resources to enhance your well-being, the following resources may be of help:

1. EFT Tapping Scripts

Explore the transformative power of EFT tapping through specialised scripts designed to enhance luck and bring you into the present moment. These scripts are meticulously crafted to guide you through the process, helping you address specific issues and align your energy with positivity.

Visit our website to access these scripts and start your tapping journey today.

2. Loving Kindness Meditation

Loving Kindness Meditation, also known as Metta Meditation, is a practice that cultivates feelings of love and compassion towards oneself and others. By incorporating this practice into your daily routine, you can develop a deeper sense of connection, empathy, and inner peace.

Explore our guided Loving Kindness Meditation to nurture your heart and soul, and spread positive vibes to the world around you.

3. Present Moment Meditation

Living in the present moment is a gift that brings profound joy and contentment. Discover the art of mindfulness through our Present Moment Meditation sessions. Our guided meditations are designed to help you ground yourself in the now, allowing you to experience life fully and authentically.

Immerse yourself in the Present Moment Meditations to cultivate a deeper sense of awareness and find tranquility amidst the chaos of everyday life.

4. Additional Resources and Support

Our website, www.lucky-collective.com is a treasure trove of resources dedicated to your well-being. Explore articles, videos, and expert advice on luck, mindfulness, and personal growth. Connect with a community of like-minded individuals, share your experiences, and learn from others on a similar journey.

Remember, seeking support is a sign of strength, and you deserve all the happiness and fulfilment life has to offer. Embrace these resources, and may your journey be filled with luck, love, and moments of pure presence.

Wishing you endless blessings on your path, Lucky Girl.

Index